GW01607438

To Grandpa,

Happy Birthday

With lots of love

from Pete, Jenny

Nick, and Tommy

Belfast.

November 1984

Spirit of the Age

The story of
"Old Bushmills"

by Alf McCreary

To
Jean Jones, Kathleen Black
and Bill McCreary.

Front Cover — View of the "Old Bushmills" Distillery across the dam.
Back Cover — 14th Century Dunluce Castle, near "Old Bushmills".

ISBN 0 9509083 0 4

Published by The "Old Bushmills" Distillery Company Ltd.

Distributed by The Blackstaff Press

Printed by The Universities Press (Belfast) Ltd.

"Books are not absolutely dead things,
but do contain a potency of life in them
to be as active as that soul was,
whose progeny they are".

John Milton, who was born in 1608, the same year as *"Old Bushmills"*.

Preface

On a particularly humid night in Guatemala, I hurried down a dark entry in a poorer part of the capital city. With me was a social worker, and we were on our way to meet a member of a leading family who had devoted himself to working for the poor. It was difficult work, and in the context of Guatemala's politics, it was also extremely dangerous. For this reason the man we wanted to see was not living like his forbears in a palatial ranch, but in a poor tenement house.

We glanced up and down the secluded alleyway before knocking softly on the door. It was opened slowly and in the pool of light there was the silhouette of a shapely woman. She invited us in, and the lamplight picked out her high cheekbones and long, blonde hair. She smiled nervously and said that her husband had been delayed, but that he would see us presently. I explained that I was carrying out research for a book about the Third World and that it was important I should find out what her husband had been trying to do for the poor.

She nodded hesitantly. Her English was halting, and my Spanish was non-existent. There was a silence. Then she beckoned towards a sideboard and asked politely if we would like a drink while we waited. I looked across. The lamplight played upon several bottles and their outlines shone against a dark mahogany background. There was bourbon from America and tequila from Mexico. But my eyes were riveted by one distinctive shape — a bottle of "Old Bushmills" whiskey. I tried to explain that both I and the whiskey came from the same place, but sign language proved to be the best form of communication, and she smiled as she handed me a tangible connection with my homeland.

The rest of the evening was spent in detailed conversation with her husband who proved to be a man of great courage and compassion. I have often wondered what happened to him in a country where life is cheap and where death can be swift; but I was left with an impression of his dedication to the poor in circumstances of extreme difficulty.

On a different level, I have often thought, too, about that bottle of "Old Bushmills" and its hint of home in a country that seemed, literally, to be a world apart. Like the Irish linen that graces homes and public places throughout the world, or the great vessels from Belfast shipyard that crossed vast oceans in an age of steam, "Old Bushmills" is an institution that is part of the fabric of this land.

Unique

When I was asked to write the story of "Old Bushmills" to mark its 375 years of existence, it was a welcome opportunity to put on record not only the distillation of a unique whiskey but also the flavour of the lives and events of nearly four centuries.

Some of that history has been available for a long time, but unfortunately a great deal of material was destroyed by a disastrous fire at "Old Bushmills" in 1885. And in 1941 the Belfast headquarters were badly damaged by the German air raids of the Second World War. An added difficulty is that successive generations of "Old Bushmills" people were not as scrupulous as they might have been in keeping documents, letters, photographs, and apparently unimportant pieces of paper. The result is that some of the historical life-blood quietly drained away. At an early point in my research it became clear that this book could not and would not be presented as the definitive history of the entire period but rather as the story of "Old Bushmills", using all the material at my disposal.

The bricks of the narrative are solid. The framework has been preserved in dusty ledgers, in forgotten envelopes lurking in ancient safes, in newspaper cuttings and advertisements, in public records, in other writings which mentioned the industry, and most important also in the recollections and anecdotes of the many human beings whose lives have been a part of the "Old Bushmills" story. The late Eoin O'Mahony, lawyer, genealogist, philosopher and Irish character, once said of a noted historian; "He was a man who knew all the bricks of history without the matrix of human beings who held them together". Happily, the matrix of "Old Bushmills" remains rich and rare.

Dynamic

This story begins with a dynamic man of fortune in the tough world of 17th century Ireland and spreads all over the globe. Today "Old Bushmills" reaches markets in more than 100 countries and the Distillery entertains multitudes of visitors, literally from Honolulu to Hull and from Boston to Brisbane. By 1784 "Old Bushmills" had established itself in North America, which became the home for many thousands of emigrants who had sailed across the North Atlantic not far from the Distillery and the rugged and beautiful Causeway Coast of North Antrim.

These links between North America and the homeland have been cemented by centuries of tradition and family ties. Appropriately, my research took me not only throughout the length and breadth of Ireland, but also to New York, Kentucky and Florida to meet the colourful American characters who are also a part of the "Old Bushmills" story.

In writing this book, I have been conscious at all times of the dividing line between moderation and excess, with regard to alcohol. It can be a social relaxant, but the dangers of misuse cannot be over-emphasised. A touchstone of ancient Greek philosophy was "Avoid excess", and the Buddha exhorted his followers to display "moderation in all things". One of the light-hearted maxims at "Old Bushmills" is that water can be beneficial when taken in the right spirit and with moderation.

It is my hope that this story of "Old Bushmills" will be taken in the right spirit as well . . .

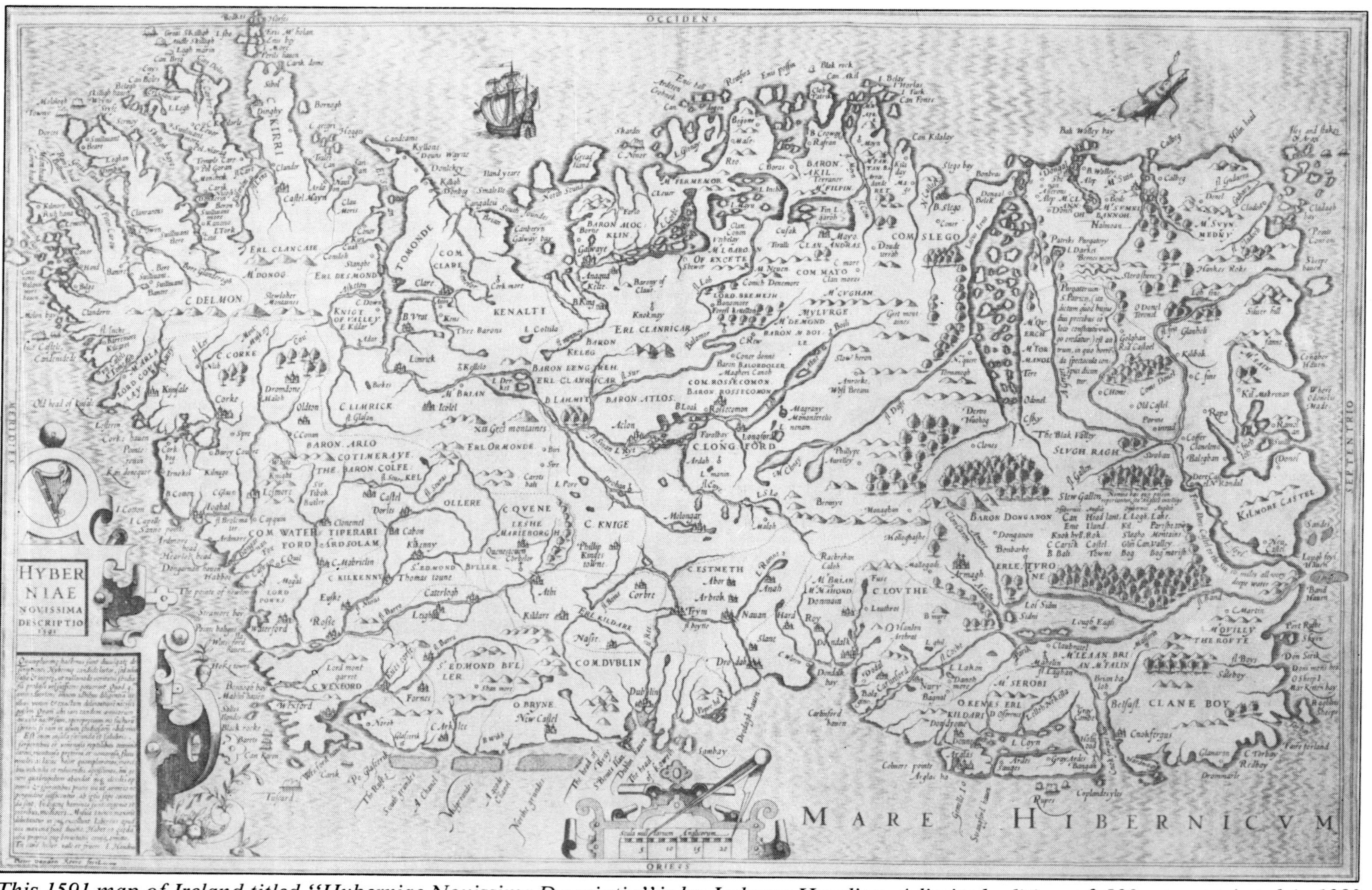

This 1591 map of Ireland titled "Hyberniae Novissima Descriptio" is by Jodocus Hondius. A limited edition of 500 was reprinted in 1983 from the copy held by the Linen Hall Library, Belfast, in association with "Old Bushmills." The map shows "the Rowte," which is featured in the distilling licence granted to Sir Thomas Phillips in 1608.

CHAPTER ONE

The World of Bushmills

"In 1608 in the village of Bushmills, a legend was born. That legend is whiskey. For in that historic year, we were granted our licence to distil."

These words which are written into an attractive wall display, snug in the depths of the Distillery at the Visitors' Reception area, are not a boast but the witness to a reality.

With typical North Antrim directness the men and women from the world of *Old Bushmills* underline their past, their present and their future. Their past moves down the mists of time to a land of legend, fair maidens and warrior chieftains. Their present is part of the world-wide story of Irish whiskey. Their future is the continued survival of timeless skills and traditions to blend with the world of the micro-chip, the computer and inter-space travel. And the golden thread of the story is the mellow whiskey of *Old Bushmills* itself, as ever the spirit of the age.

In 1608 when the craftsmen of Bushmills began to distil whiskey under licence it was the world of the mature Galileo and the infant Milton. Elizabeth I had been dead only five years. Shakespeare was alive and had written King Lear and Macbeth, Antony and Cleopatra, Coriolanus and Timon of Athens, during the three years from 1605. In 1608 the first cheques or 'cash letters' were in use in the Netherlands. In London the Royal Blackheath Golf Club, still in existence, was founded. Two years earlier Guy Fawkes and his fellow conspirators were sentenced to death for trying to blow up Parliament buildings during the State opening by King James I.

A mere 116 years earlier, Christopher Columbus had discovered the New World. In the year of *Old Bushmills*, Samuel de Champlain founded the city of Quebec. In September 1608 John Smith, the explorer and principal founder of the first permanent English settlement in North America at Jamestown, became president of the colony. Barrels of *Old Bushmills* were maturing in dark stores years before the Dutch settled Manhattan Island and before New Amsterdam became New York. *Old Bushmills* was given the official seal of approval some 30 years before Harvard was founded in the United States, and nearly a century before Yale.

History

In the broad sweep of European history, the Czar Boris Gudunov of Russia died just three years before *Old Bushmills* was born. It was nurtured in a world of

Downhill — and in the distance a beautiful beach with the poetic name, Magilligan, that is so typical of the outstanding beauty of the coastline near Bushmills.

Monteverdi and Rembrandt. It grew up in the Europe of battles and tortuous alliances, and the splendour and decadence of the court of Louis XIV of France, the "Sun King" who was the symbol of absolute monarchy in a classic age. It was an age which has something to say to the world of today — when an Italian chemist offered Louis XIV the first bacteriological weapon, the King gave him a pension on condition that he would never divulge his invention.

Nearer home there was continued unrest. History records the "Flight of the Earls" in 1607 from Ireland to Europe, following the failure of their insurrection. The Ireland of today still fails to find peace with itself. In that respect, so little has changed.

Fortunately little has changed too in the distillation and production of Bushmills whiskeys. To this day the water is drawn from a stream known as St. Columb's Rill which rises in bogland some five miles from the Distillery and flows across peat and basalt to absorb its distinctive flavour. It is named after the missionary saint who taught the Gospels far and wide. It is possible that St. Patrick himself breathed the same air of Antrim in his days of slavery as he tended sheep at Slemish, not far away.

St. Columb

Many years later, water from the same St. Columb's Rill is heated and mixed with malted barley. Yeast is then added to create fermentation. At a later stage the liquid is distilled and the transformation to malt whiskey begins. *Old Bushmills* is distilled three times before being drawn off at a crucial stage in the process which has remained a trade secret down the centuries. The strength of this clear liquid is decreased by specially treated water before it is filled into carefully chosen oak casks to mature.

This maturation is a mystery of nature and of time itself. In the slow darkness of the years, the clear liquid takes on a golden colour and in the fullness of time the casks are taken back to the light of day where the blender draws on his traditional skills to produce whiskeys as distinctive as their flavours are unchanged. Some of the details of production have been modernised, but in essence it is time that has moved with *Old Bushmills*. Good taste in every age remains the same.

The geographical world of *Old Bushmills* has changed little also, throughout the wind and the weather of the centuries. It is near one of the glories of European landscape, the North Antrim coast. On stormy days the wild Atlantic hurls itself against the cracks and fissures and the beaches and boulders of sturdy headlands and hidden coves. But on soft, summer evenings the green of hillsides blends with the dark Atlantic blues and this North Coast world of Bushmills is full of warmth and light.

Magilligan

To the west is the mouth of Lough Foyle and the beautiful beach with the poetic name, Magilligan Strand. It was on this beach that one of the more unusual races in history took place, in the latter part of the 18th century. The story is told of Frederick Hervey, Bishop of Derry and 4th Earl of Bristol, who entertained a number of Presbyterians as well as his own clergy to dinner one evening in his resplendent mansion on top of nearby cliffs.

The Earl-Bishop suggested that they take advantage of the fine summer weather with a stroll along the strand. The guests were somewhat surprised to find the Earl's servants advancing across the sand with saddled horses. To their consternation his Lordship announced that they would have a contest — namely a race between the Anglican Church and the Presbyterians, and that he himself would act as Starter. Posterity records that the Presbyterians won, possibly because of a more Puritanical disposition which elevates clean, healthy living to a virtue. To this day the spectacle of lean and corpulent men of God racing on horseback across the sand adds a touch of warm humanity to this story of the richest, and arguably the most eccentric, churchman in 18th century Ireland.

The Earl-Bishop, despite his worldly ways, was noted for his simple acts of charity to the poor and for his piety on the appropriate occasion — Charles Wesley noted that he could deliver 'a useful sermon' and that he 'celebrated the Lord's Supper with admirable solemnity'. But he is better remembered today for his architectural

Frederick Hervey, Bishop of Derry and 4th Earl of Bristol. One of his eccentricities was to stage a race on horseback between Anglican and Presbyterian clergymen on Downhill Strand.

visions of grand design. His Downhill Castle was built around 1780 and had commanding views of the Irish and Scottish coasts. Today it is a ruin, but Mussenden Temple, completed in 1785 on the very edge of the cliffs, has weathered well the ravages of time and is also the property of the National Trust. It was named after his cousin the beautiful Mrs. Mussenden and was inspired by the temples of Vesta at Tivoli in Rome. (The Earl-Bishop's contemporaries were not amused and thought this to be inappropriate conduct by a Bishop whose wife had just left him).

Portstewart

After such stories of clerical exotica it is almost a relief to travel further along the coast to the neat, some would say reserved, town of Portstewart with its bracing views of North Donegal. Portstewart has its own rich character and history. Charles

Mussenden Temple on the edge of steep cliffs with breathtaking views — and memories of a beautiful lady and a whiff of local scandal.

Lever, the distinguished Irish novelist, lived there in the early 19th century, and one of his guests was the celebrated English writer William Makepeace Thackeray. It was also the home temporarily in the early part of this century of the well-known Irish songwriter Jimmy Kennedy who produced "Red Sails in the Sunset". To the east are the more worldly delights of Portrush, with its championship golf course which staged the British Open in 1951. Experts in this difficult art say that Portrush golf course has some of the best holes in the world, lying sweetly and innocently among the bracken. In fact the entire area around Bushmills has an abundance of good courses.

The North Coast on its good days can shine like a jewel in the bright sun, but its furious storms and treacherous seas can strike terror in the heart of man. It was on one such night in October 1588 that the Spanish galleass Girona, limping home from the defeat of the Spanish Armada, foundered on North Antrim shores. She was part of the pride of a fleet sent by Philip II of Spain to conquer the England of Elizabeth I.

Portstewart-links with the world famous "Red Sails in the Sunset" and superb vistas across the sea to County Donegal.

The Girona and her sister vessels sailed to defeat by the English under Sir Francis Drake, who gave bowls as well as seamanship a place in folklore and history. The rest of the story was sheer disaster for the Spanish. The Girona carried the combined equipment and the riches of five other Armada vessels. At dawn on October 27, the Girona sank off Lacada Point. Only five men out of 1,300 survived.

Some 400 years later a team of Belgian and French divers recovered the submerged treasure including cannons, gold and silver plate, valuable coins and gorgeous rubies, diamonds and pearls. These had been in the ocean only 20 years when *Old Bushmills*, just a few miles away, was granted its first licence. Today remnants of that Spanish treasure enrich the Ulster Museum in Belfast, where they are on permanent display.

Dunluce

The Girona foundered near Dunluce. Here stands a roofless yet dignified castle that has been the custodian of the years and the survivor of countless storms, political and otherwise. Dating from around 1300, Dunluce Castle has withstood sieges and wars in the bad times, and enjoyed banquets and carousing in the good. In 1639, in the generation when the first of *Old Bushmills* had not long come of age, one such night had an unfortunate climax. During a severe storm part of the kitchen fell into the sea, carrying with it a number of servants.

Today Dunluce Castle, like *Old Bushmills* itself, remains one of the landmarks of

A Galleass of the Spanish Armada. In 1588 The Girona foundered off the North Antrim Coast, just 20 years before "Old Bushmills" itself was launched.

Treasure on the sea-bed. A Gold Salamander pendant set with rubies, and the most spectacular item from the jewellery of The Girona.

Dunluce Castle, a roofless yet dignified building dating from the 14th century — and its story of disaster on a stormy night in 1639.

Dunseverick — back to Tara, the ancient Royal capital of Ireland, and a legend dating from the Crucifixion.

Ballintoy Harbour — a quaintness not unlike Devon or Cornwall or even Brittany.

the North. But perhaps the greatest physical landmark, just three miles from the Distillery, is the Giant's Causeway, which has been rightly described as one of the wonders of the world. It is a vista of cliffs and breathtaking columns of basalt formed some 60 million years ago by the cooling and shrinking of molten lava. The key of geology can unlock its history, but in the rare Irish atmosphere of language and vivid imagination it is surrounded by legends as attractive as they are improbable.

It is said that the Irish giant Finn McCool built the Causeway in order to walk over to Scotland without getting wet! As so often happens in Ireland, there is a glimmer of truth in the legend. Similar geological structures can be seen on the Scottish island of Staffa in the Hebrides. Another version is that Finn McCool wanted to fight a Scottish giant and they built a causeway to reach a common meeting-place. The Scot's huge reputation went before him, so Finn McCool disguised himself in child's clothing and his wife pretended that the 'father' was elsewhere. The Scottish giant returned home in a rage and on his way back threw pieces of the causeway into the sea, so that today it is visible only at each end. Such legends are not surprising. Why indeed should facts be allowed to spoil a good story!

Dunseverick

Like Dunluce, another ancient castle along the coast has its foundations set deep into the history of the region. Dunseverick is the northern point of the road from Tara, the ancient Royal capital of Ireland in the Celtic age, and was once a main port for the voyage to Scotland. According to legend, a Dunseverick man who served in the Roman Army was a witness at Christ's Crucifixion. Dunseverick Castle itself had a turbulent history and there were many battles between the local chieftains of the Macdonnells, the O'Neills and the O'Cahans.

Medieval history, colourful though it was, pales into its own perspective against the antiquity of White Park Bay, further to the east. It is thought that this area was first inhabited around 2500 BC by Neolithic man, who used flints from the chalk to make arrowheads and other tools. At Bushmills itself a souterrain was discovered in 1973 when excavations were being made in preparation for building more warehouses. A company spokesman at the time said; "It indicates that centuries ago, back possibly to the 5th century, there was a settlement at Bushmills with underground tunnels for the protection of wives and families against marauding fighters seeking cattle, mainly as war prizes".

If history abounds along the North coast, so too does its remarkable beauty. The little village of Ballintoy, with a quaintness not unlike Devon or Cornwall or indeed Brittany is enticing to the tourist and day-tripper alike.

Out to sea lies Rathlin Island where Robert the Bruce of Scotland hid after his defeat in 1306 by the English. He watched a spider in his cave repeatedly try to reach the roof, until it eventually succeeded. He was inspired by its determination, and with consummate tenacity and the will to "try, try again" he returned to regain the Scottish throne at Bannockburn.

Ballintoy

In these waters too, the Vikings ploughed their strange longboats, but there were also men of peace. St. Columb himself sailed past this very coast with his followers as they brought the light of Christianity to Scotland and to dark Europe beyond.

Other men of peace chart similar currents today as they reap the harvest of the sea. Salmon fishermen know every inlet and eddy. At Carrick-a-Rede they cross a sea-gorge from high cliffs by means of wooden planks with rope handrails. It is a venture that needs steady nerves and a head for heights. The superb views are always a compensation.

To complete the semi-circle to the east, there is the picturesque town of Ballycastle. In August each year it is the focus for the Ould Lammas Fair. The Lammas (Loaf-Mass) dates from medieval times when each August the first wheat was made into flour, and the first bread was used at Mass in the local church. Today the Ould Lammas Fair still thrives and attracts large numbers of people to enjoy such local delights as 'dulse' (dried seaweed) and a sticky sweet called "yellow man".

Bushmills

Thus in this broad semi-circle from the ruggedness of Magilligan and Mussenden to the beauty of Ballintoy and the rich character of Ballycastle there is a wealth of landscape, history, and legend. And at the heart of this is Bushmills, within easy reach of all these tourist delights. It is small wonder that the Distillery has become a firm favourite with visitors keen to combine history, scenic beauty and relaxation and many thousands of people pass through the Visitors' Centre at Bushmills each year.

Many come from Northern Ireland and the Irish Republic, but the range is remarkable geographically. On one wall of the Potstill Bar, which houses many of the treasured souvenirs and historical memorabilia of the Distillery, there is a large world map with coloured pins. Each pin denotes a visitor or group from a particular country. The list has an impressive international flavour.

It includes Honolulu, Alaska, Canada, Mexico, the USA, Honduras, Panama, Venezuela, Barbados, Chile, Bermuda, Greenland, Iceland, the United Kingdom, France, Belgium, West Germany, Spain, Portugal, Italy, Poland, Czechoslovakia, Hungary, Austria, Romania, Greece, Turkey, Iran, Russia, Mongolia, Afghanistan, Nepal, India, Thailand, Vietnam, China, Hong-Kong, Japan, Phillipines, Malaysia, New Guinea, Australia, Morocco, Libya, Egypt, Israel, Kuwait, Saudi Arabia, Sierra Leone, Ivory Coast, Ghana, Nigeria, Sudan, Kenya, Zimbabwe, Malawi and South Africa. There are visitors literally from Anchorage to Athens and from Dundee to Dunedin.

The Giant's Causeway, near "Old Bushmills", which is a famous landmark. It has been described rightly as one of the physical wonders of the world.

International

This impressive list of local and international visitors is an accurate reflection of the increasing world penetration of Bushmills products. At one time it served a largely local market, with limited exports to Britain, the United States and Canada. In the old days the Distillery could produce whiskey only when barley was available for malting. This was a seasonal activity — a good season would last from the harvest around October until May or June. In a poor season with limited supplies of barley the work in the Distillery might cease at the end of April.

The aptly-named silent season lasted from early or late Spring until the autumn. During this period some workers were retained to carry out maintenance work and to keep the Distillery and its surrounds spruced and tidy. Other workers found employment on the land or in association with local tourism, and a number worked on the local tramway each summer. It was a neat example of man adapting to his social and natural environment at a time when Nature dictated patterns of employment.

With the development of the huge, modern maltings the "silent season" has been reduced to four weeks annual holiday, and the output has increased accordingly. The *Old Bushmills* Distillery has the capacity to produce about one million gallons annually for a market of over 100 countries worldwide with particular emphasis on Ireland north and south, the USA and Canada, Britain, Germany, France, Finland, Italy and the Far East.

Markets

Understandably this widespread market and vastly increased production has been made possible by modern business techniques and management. In this respect the Distillery has changed vastly from 1608 when the first licence was granted to Sir Thomas Phillipps to make 'aquavitae in the County of Colrane and the Route, Co. Antrim'.

In 1784 the Distillery became an officially registered company, and at that stage it was exporting whiskey to America and the West Indies. The owners claimed subsequently that the first legalised Distillery was the property of Hugh Anderson. Officially recorded information about the Distillery at this time is sketchy. There is evidence of one owner paying duty on a large consignment in the early part of the 19th century, and a number of legal documents later on testify to the business changing hands several times. In 1885 the existing buildings were destroyed by fire, though a subscription list of 1891 made it clear that the Distillery had been rebuilt "and is now in first-class working order".

The Distllery not only survived but prospered during the First World War and under the steady hand of the Boyd family, with headquarters in Belfast, the business made a distinct mark on the commercial life of Northern Ireland. With Wilson

The distillery dam, containing the precious water from St. Columb's Rill, remains beautifully landscaped — and brings out the best in photographers.

Boyd, a man of determination and strong character, at the helm the company also prospered during the Second World War despite the unwelcome attention of the German Luftwaffe which badly damaged the Hill Street headquarters during an air-raid.

Changing

After the war, however, the company which had been so identified with one family changed hands. It was bought in 1947 by Isaac Wolfson of Great Universal Stores, and seventeen years later it was acquired by Charringtons. In 1972 it changed hands again and was purchased by the Seagram Company Ltd., of Montreal, the world's largest producer of distilled spirits and wines.

In 1976 the Seagram Company obtained a twenty per cent holding in Irish Distillers and as part of an agreement shortly afterwards *Old Bushmills* itself became a wholly owned subsidiary of Irish Distillers Group. Thus bringing it back once again into Irish ownership. Within this group The *Old Bushmills* Distillery Co. Ltd., retains its own identity.

That distinct character of *Old Bushmills* is evident physically. The vast increases in output have led to new warehouses but, happily for conservationists, they are not an intrusion upon the rural beauty of County Antrim. It is still possible to note a dappled cow among the buttercups at the edge of the Distillery and to hear the Spring skylark in the clear air. The local dam, containing the precious water from St. Columb's Rill, remains beautifully landscaped and has inspired countless photographs. At one time a flock of geese enhanced that soothing vista (and kept the weeds down as well) but their nocturnal cackling outweighed their usefulness, and the dam is now picturesquely silent.

Old Bushmills is also distinctive because it is one of the few locations where distilling, blending and bottling are combined under the one roof. In many Scottish distilleries, for example, the only activity is the production of malt whiskey which is then transported elsewhere for the delicate process of blending.

Blending

The Bushmills Distillery is essentially a blend between the old and the new. At the heart of the Still Room with its huge and gleaming copper stills is the control panel which resembles the bridge of a huge liner with its complex-looking controls, coloured lights and diagrams. Yet outside, the Bushmills yard has hardly changed for generations. It is still a picture of weathered stone and tile, with large areas of wood painted a striking red, and walls brightly white-washed.

Towering over all, and unchanged for the greater part of this century are the twin Pagoda Towers which give the *Old Bushmills* landscape more than a hint of the mysterious East. They are now largely decorative, as the barley is no longer dried at Bushmills. In their heyday the Towers acted as chimneys for the old kilns and they needed a large aperture to allow the moisture-laden vapour to escape. The tops of the towers were curved to prevent rain from getting in. They also act as a lightning conductor. The towers date from the early part of this century but though they have largely outlived their practical usefulness they remain an architectural treasure. *Old Bushmills* would not look the same without them.

The Towers are indeed a landmark that is obvious to all. Rather more subtle but of vital importance is *Old Bushmills*' most enduring asset — the people who have spent their lives in and around the Distillery. They are modest folk who often make a few words go a long way. But there is a quiet pride in craftsmanship and in producing something that is not made in quite the same way anywhere else in the world.

That pride and craftsmanship can be detected relatively easily. For many years the

Distillery has produced two brands of whiskey — its light-gold ''*Old Bushmills*'', and its darker, older and more expensive ''Black Bush''. On occasions a stranger may be heard to ask in the hospitality room for a glass, not of ''Black Bush'', but of ''ordinary Bushmills''. When that happens there is a polite but a definite silence. Then comes the reply, as slow but as sure as a Bushmills man himself; ''There's no such thing as 'ordinary Bushmills'. There's only 'Good' and 'Better' Bushmills!'' The point about the Bushmills man is that he really means it!

The Pagoda Towers — a Bushmills landmark with more than a hint of the mysterious East.

CHAPTER TWO

Ages of Bushmills

The town of Bushmills has its roots in the 17th century with the arrival of Scottish families during the Plantation of Ulster but references to the River Bush itself are found much further back in history. It was long regarded as one of the "king-waters" of Ireland ('rigusci Erend') and it is mentioned in "Lebor na hUidre" — the Book of the Dun Cow dating from about 1100 AD.

This is an old Irish story, indeed a kind of Macbeth tragedy. The hero is fighting so strenuously that he develops a great thirst and a friend tours Ireland to try to get him water to drink. But the 'evil spirits' dry up all the rivers as he approaches them. The name of the friend is Mac Cécht.

He ". . . set out then and he went first to the well of Casar which was nearby in the Dublin-Bray area, but he was unable to fill the cup with water from it (the gold cup Conaire put into his hand.) Before morning he had visited in turn all the king-waters of Ireland i.e.
Bush
Boyne,
Bann,
Barrow,
Blackwater, (Cork)
Lee,
Bandon (Cork)
Shannon,
Suir,
Sligo,
Erne,
Finn (Donegal),
Liffey,
and had failed to fill the cup with water from them. He proceeded then to the principal lakes . . . before morning and failed again. He went then to the Spring of Gara in Co. Roscommon. This Spring was unable to hide itself from him, so he filled the cup from it, and the cup went under his protection. Whereupon he got back to Dá Derga's Hostel before morning."[1]

It is interesting to note that the Bush is first on the list, the Boyne is second, and the poor old Liffey — the pride of Dublin — is last!

Ancient

One of the most authoritative books on the entire area is "The Causeway Coast" by Julia E. Mullin.[2] She notes that some facts are known about the early churches in the two parishes where Bushmills is situated — that is, Billy to the east of the River Bush and Dunluce to the west. "The ancient church of Billy was not where modern Bushmills lies, but was in the centre of the parish (where there is today an episcopalian church and an old graveyard) and apparently was a church of considerable importance, for in the Taxation of Pope Nicholas (c. 1306) it was valued at £36, which was the highest valuation of any church in the diocese."[3]

The parish of Dunluce was unusual because it had two early Roman Catholic Churches — one at Dunluce and one at Portcamon on the west bank of the Bush "where the Episcopalian Church of St. Cuthbert's now stands. In the taxation of Pope Nicholas, Dunluce is valued at 47s 4d." The church at Portcamon was valued at £8-10-8 in 1306 so it would appear to be the more important of the two in the parish. Mrs. Mullin also notes "The name Portcamon seems to have been retained until early in the 17th century, when the mills on the river Bush led to the name Bushmills. These mills and a crossing of the river led to a few cabins being built, but it was not until about 200 years later that Bushmills developed into a town."[4]

The Bushmills Distillery began its life officially in a Province that was recovering from the after-effects of the Tudor conquest and the ravages of war. Professor J. C. Beckett in his standard work "The Making of Modern Ireland 1603-1923" gives a fascinating, if sobering, glimpse of the rigours of life in the Ulster of these early days.

"Ulster had few towns of any sort. It was still the most thoroughly Gaelic part of the country, and the Gaelic social system did not conduce to urban life or commercial activity. Besides this, the province had suffered severely under the later stages of the Elizabethan wars. Inland towns could hardly be said to exist. When the deputy and his train toured the inland parts of Ulster in 1606 they found no settled lodging; even when they stopped in the neighbourhood of what passed for a town (as, for example, at Cavan) they slept in their tents; and in the whole of the county of Fermanagh they could find nowhere to hold the assizes but a ruined monastery, temporarily fitted up for the purpose."

"External trade amounted to very little. There was, and had long been, some intercourse between the north-western coast and Spain, fish being exported in exchange for wine; but the trade was not great enough for the development of seaports. The old ports of the north-east, relics of Anglo-Norman settlement in the twelfth century, had only a local importance; the chief of them, Carrickfergus, had little to boast of save its antiquity, its castle, and its unswerving allegiance to the crown. Two of the garrisons planted during the Tudor period, Newry and Derry, were well-placed for trade; and though of small account in the opening years of the century, they soon shared in the economic development that followed the establishment of peace."

Few Roads

"Since the main centres of population lay along the coast, communication between them could be maintained by sea; but inland communication was slow and difficult. The rivers, though interrupted by fords, weirs and cataracts, provided the best means of transport for heavy goods; it was, for example, the woodlands lying along the great rivers of Munster that were most quickly and profitably exploited. But there were few roads capable of taking wheeled traffic, and in many areas there were no roads at all; rural Ireland was much more self-contained than rural England.

"The English or continental traveller found that Irish urban life followed, though with sharp local variations, the general pattern to which he was accustomed; but if he ventured beyond the towns he was in a strange land indeed. The dwellings of the people — little villages of round, wattled huts without chimneys, like 'so many hives of bees about a farm'; their costume; their diet, which contained little bread and no beer, but great quantities of curdled milk — in all this he could find matter for astonishment, or even for disgust. But traveller after traveller remarks on the richness of the soil and the possibility of development; and the ruins with which the countryside was dotted — churches, abbeys, castles — bore witness to a greater prosperity in the past. Before the end of James I's reign, the first signs of recovery had begun to appear."[5]

That was in 1625, and as the century wore on conditions improved — certainly for the merchants, and particularly in the North, where the linen industry was flourishing. W. R. Hutchison in "Two Centuries of Irish History" states; "Dublin was, of course, the capital city of Ireland and the centre of social as well as political and business life. In 1765 it had about 120,000 inhabitants. Cork at the same date had 60,000, Limerick, 25,000 and Belfast a mere 8,000. But as the century wore on Belfast rapidly became the centre of a thriving industrial area and by the end of the century its population had trebled."[6]

If life was agreeable for the landowning and merchant classes it was rather less so for the ordinary people. Conditions in the north were better than in other parts of Ireland, partly due to the Northern weaving industry and also to Ulster Tenant Right — a custom by which the peasant had certain privileges. These included the right to stay on his holding, provided his rent was paid, and also the right to receive compensation for certain improvements made. Nevertheless, life in the 18th century was hard, with little or no luxuries.

Such conditions would have applied to the area around Bushmills, as elsewhere in Ulster, though the Distillery would have provided some employment and therefore an amelioration of certain of the hardships of life. Details of the town in these years are by no means plentiful, and Julia Mullin notes that "Until the 19th century the main facts which are obtainable about Bushmills concern the mills and the landlords of the district."[7]

She writes "A beautiful map, made about 1750, shows the townlands of Airds, Ballymoy, Karnkark, Killcubin, Castlenagree, Clogher, Park and Bushmills, totalling 1102 acres which had been leased to John McCollum by the Earl of Antrim. The map was drawn by Roger Sheridan at the request of Hugh McCollum. This map shows thatched cottages and trees in each townland, with a two-storied house to the east of Bushmills, sailing boats off the coast and rowing boats near the shore at the Giant's Causeway (townland of Airds), the whole enclosed in an elaborate border of flowers, but unfortunately it does not illustrate the part of the property containing the mills. Unfortunately, too, Roger Sheridan, while producing a most attractive map, does not seem to have been portraying existing conditions, as he drew 3 cottages in each townland and in Bushmills put a large chapel and 3 houses along the road."[8] Mrs. Mullin states that she found no evidence of a chapel on the east side of the River Bush at that time.

Sources for the Bushmills area are rather more plentiful in the 19th century, and the Belfast Monthly Magazine of August 1813 gives a colourful description of a "Sketch of a Tour to Carrick-a-Rede Bridge." The writer states "Dunluce Castle is a monument of more than Feudal greatness; built in a rude age, it is void of much ornament, but bold in the plan, and difficult in its execution. It was evidently designed for a place of strength, in that age in which this unhappy country was divided into petty clans, continually disputing with one another, about their pretended rights and injuries, or for the purposes of rapine and plunder".[9]

". . . An old man, whom we met after coming across the bridge from the ruins of the castle, showed us the apartments which were occupied by the Duchess of Buckingham, who lived here some time in the reign of Elizabeth. But whether his information be correct, or not, we had not the means of ascertaining. Being satisfied with the view we had got of the ruins, we descended the rock to see the cave which

Dunluce Castle from the west. This is from Statistical Survey of the County of Antrim, by John Dubourdieu, Dublin 1812. The original drawing is by Holt Waring.

Carrick-a-Rede Bridge, from Ireland Illustrated, edited by G. N. Wright, London 1833. The print is dated 1831 and it shows salmon fishing in progress.

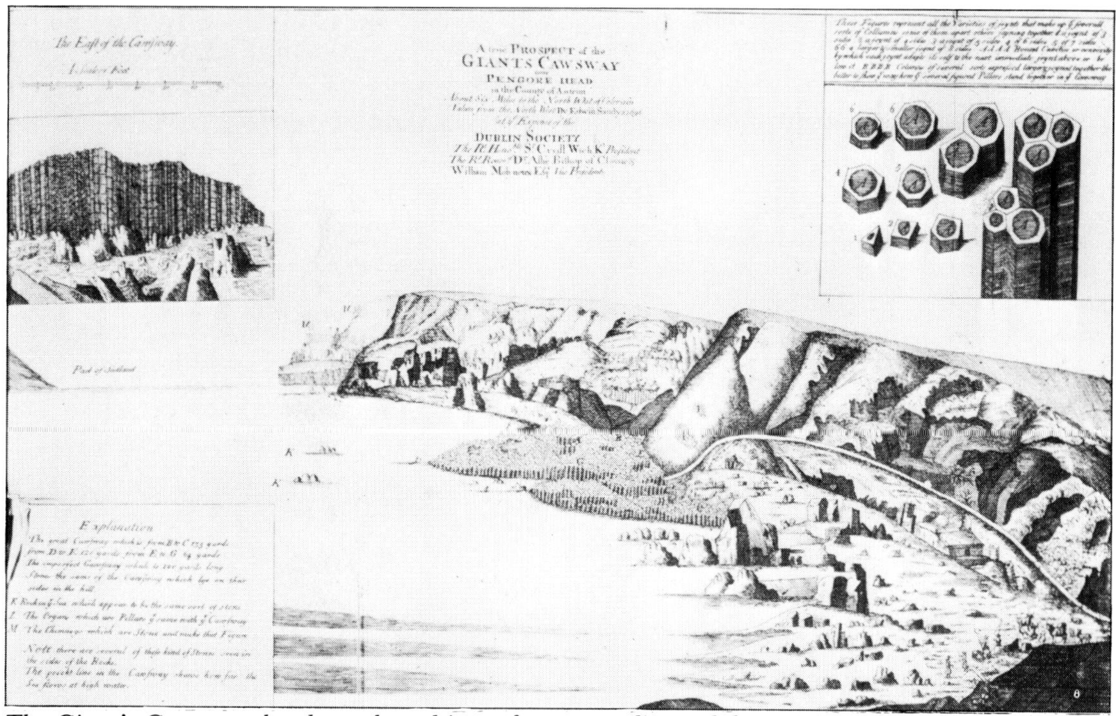

The Giant's Causeway has been the subject of many studies and drawings. This is one of the earliest views — "A true prospect of the Giants Cawsway" from A Natural History of Ireland by G. Boate, Dublin 1726. The print was originally drawn by Edwin Sandys in 1696.

passes under the castle, through the rock to the sea. Having descended in the cavern as far as the verge of the sea, we began to exercise our voices, and throw stones into the water, for the purpose of witnessing the re-echoing properties of the enormous arch which extended itself above us. Our curiosity being gratified with the scenery which the cave presented, and being refreshed by the cool shade which the place afforded, with considerable difficulty we again clambered up the rock, and got upon the same road by which we had entered."[10]

Suitably refreshed, the writer and his party proceed to Portballintrae. "Without having observed anything of importance on the road, we arrived at Port-Ballintray in less than half-an-hour, a distance from Dunluce of about one mile. There are a number of houses built along the margin of the bay, chiefly occupied by lodgers from the neighbouring towns, who retire to this place during the summer months for the purpose of bathing. We walked around to the eastern side of the Bay, from which there is a fine view of Seaport, an elegant modern building in the style of the Scotch villas, presenting a front in three directions. There is a gravelled walk which extends to a considerable distance in the rear of the building, along the rock heads, from which there is a good view of the white rocks, with their natural arches, the mouth of Derry Lough, and the adjacent head-lands."

"Finding nothing more in this place to interest our attention, we continued our journey to Bush-mills, a small village, one mile distant from the place we had last visited, and two from the Giant's Causeway. The day being very pleasant, after having refreshed ourselves at the inn, we continued our route to the Giant's Causeway."

And all this rural Irish delight only a year after Napoleon's retreat from Moscow, and two years before his defeat by Wellington at Waterloo. In the Europe of 1813, composers Verdi and Richard Wagner were born. So too were the missionary David Livingstone and Danish philosopher Kierkegaard. In the same year Jane Austen wrote "Pride and Prejudice". In the America of 1814 the British burned Washington, and a year later the Americans defeated the British at the Battle of New Orleans.

Richest

One of the richest sources of information about Bushmills in the 19th century is the Ordnance Survey Memoirs, preserved by the Royal Irish Academy in Dublin. The report of August, 1835 on the parish of Billy is detailed and illuminating. "Bushmills until about 8 years ago almost entirely consisted of a few cabins of an inferior description. It is not accurately known when it was originally built or what determined its site, but it is supposed that the corn mills and bridge over the River Bush formed a sort of nucleus for the cabins and cottages."

Bushmills consisted of one principal street, exactly 729 yards from south to north. "From this a smaller one branches in a westerly direction and extends over the Bush with Dunluce parish. Except 4, the houses in the latter street are all one storey and of an inferior description. Bushmills contains 154 houses of which 3 are 3 storey, 78 are 2 storey, and the rest 1 storey cabins. All are built of stone and except for the cabins

Dundarave, Co. Antrim, the home of the Macnaghten family who have played a prominent role in the story of Bushmills.

are mostly all slated. The principal street is of tolerable breadth and becoming rather uniform as the old cabins are removed and new houses built."

The town had a Presbyterian "meeting-house", rebuilt in 1825, a Methodist chapel built with funds raised by public subscription a year later, and the Parish Church was in a townland some three-quarters of a mile to the south. There was also a three-storey Courthouse, a neat building standing near the centre of the main street. "It was built by Sir Francis Macnaghten, the proprietor of the town who fitted up the second floor as a court for holding petty sessions. One room is fitted up on the first floor as a sort of bridewell."

Sir Francis was also responsible for building the market-place in 1828. "It consists of an enclosure 158 feet by 88 feet, with two gates on the side next the street. A commodious slated shed extends across it from front to rear, and affords protection to the grain offered for sale in wet weather. The Saving Bank also is held here in a house fitted up for the purpose, and the Public crane is also erected in it."

There were two markets each week — the larger on Tuesday and the other on a Friday. The former began on September 16, 1828. "The market on a Friday is very small and inconsiderable. The articles actually sold are meal, potatoes, and a little grain and a little yarn. A linen market was established in 1833, but was very soon given up."

Annual

There were four annual fairs — on 28th March, 28th June, 22nd October and 12th December. "Horses and cattle of all kinds are sold at these farms and in considerable numbers. The former are not of a very superior quality — these with pedlars goods, crockery and a few other articles constitute all the commodities brought for sale — very few cattle are brought up for exportation. They are all the

"Swinging Bridge" — this study of a post-Edwardian lady on Carrick-a-Rede by William Alfred Green dates from around 1918. Green lived from 1870 to 1958 and served his time with R. J. Welch, the major Ulster photographer of that period. Green set up his own business about 1910 and was noted for his outstanding studies of rural life. A good account of the work of both men, and of early Ulster photography is contained in Brian Mercer Walker's "Shadows on Glass", published by The Appletree Press, Belfast, in 1976. Welch is also featured in "Ireland's Eye", edited by E. E. Evans and B. S. Turner and published by Blackstaff Press.

A modern view of Carrick-a-Rede from below. The bridge made from planks with handrails is used by salmon fishermen to cross a deep gorge. It requires a good head for heights, but the views are superb.

produce of the neighbouring farms and are brought by the carts of the farmers. No tolls or customs are levied."

There seemed to be no major shortage of food. "Bushmills is tolerably well supplied with meat, poultry, eggs, milk, vegetables and small fruit, also butter. Meat is sometimes rather scarce in Spring."[11] It is all the more depressing that just ten years later Ireland was ravaged by famine, in one of the darkest periods of her history. The failure of the potato crop, a staple diet, and widespread disease led to mass deaths and large-scale emigration by which some one and a half million people set out for North America.

Back in 1835 however, Bushmills like the North-East was prospering. It had a hotel, and "two small inns", as well as the sturdy arm of the law — "there is a two-storey house in the principal street fitted up as a police barracks," with accommodation for four men. The town also had a spade and shovel factory and, of course, the Distillery which is singled out for special mention. "The character of the Bushmills Whiskey stands very high in every part of Ireland." Thus, some 227 years after being granted its official licence *Old Bushmills* seems to have established itself firmly as part of the wider Irish social scene.

The Ordnance Survey Memoirs also record in 1835; "It is in contemplation to establish a brewery and tannery as soon as possible. Outside the town there are flax mills in the parishes of Eagry and Ardihannon." (There were also mills on the western side of the river but these are not mentioned because they were in the neighbouring parish of Dunluce.)

The tone of the report on Bushmills is decidely positive. "Bushmills has improved rapidly during the last 7 years and still continues to improve — owing to the exertions of the proprietor Sir Francis Workman Macnaghten who built the markets, stores etc before mentioned, besides several good houses for persons in residence, dealers etc to whom he offered encouragement to settle there. The business and dealing in Bushmills is all increasing. The numbers who visit it on their way to the Giant's Causeway contribute not only to the support of the hotel keepers but also to that of the dealers and guides. Families are more in habit of coming to the neighbouring coast for bathing during the summer months, and Sir Francis now having made Bushmills his fixed residence must from his large income and establishment, and the employment he afforded to artisans and labourers, contribute much towards its prosperity and improvement."

Prosperity

Sir Francis evidently had made a good impression not only on Bushmills but also on the writer of the Survey! However, there were other sound reasons for such increasing prosperity. "The market built by Sir Francis Macnaghten affords a nearer and more convenient market to the farmers and there are few parishes possessing a greater advantage, namely a good grain market and storage within four miles of a harbour — Portrush — where grain, butter etc may be shipped weekly for England and Scotland."

Bushmills at this time was well-endowed with schools, and no less than ten are listed for the district. "The establishment of schools has led to a perceptible improvement in the moral habits of the people and in nothing more than the observance of the Sabbath. They are very anxious to have their children read and write, and there are few of 15 years of age who cannot read. They are very desirous of information and knowledge, and this has been encouraged by the establishment of a religious tract and Book society in the town..."

On the darker side of life, there was no regular provision for the poor. "There are but few poor in the parish, but in the summer many come from inland parishes." In general there was also health care, and a dispensary was established in 1830. The author of the Survey takes a lofty view of the people of Bushmills at that time.

"The inhabitants of this parish are like those of all the adjacent ones, descendents of the Scottish and English settlers (principally the former) who came over in the reign of James I. The present inhabitants retain the dialect and much of the usages and habits of their forefathers.

"The people are peaceable, orderly and well-conducted. Theft or ordered crime being wholly unknown in the parish. They are industrious, obliging and hospitable, and are generally comfortable in their circumstances. The houses of the lower classes are all one-storey and built of stone and slate, and generally consist of a kitchen and sleeping apartment.

"Those on the eastern side of the parish, particularly along the edge of the large tract of bog are rather of an inferior description, being inhabited by the poorer classes who settle there because of their proximity to firing, which next to food is their greatest comfort. There are several very comfortable farmhouses on the western and northern sides of the parish, about some of which there is a good deal of taste and neatness. The houses of the lower class are rather clearly and comfortable, and receive light from at least two glazed windows."

Long-lived

"Meal potatoes, milk and a little bacon and some fish constitute their food. Salt herrings are much used by the poorer class. Tea is now in regular use, and bread in considerable demand. Turf is their only fuel, and it is very abundant. They are rather long-lived and healthy, and do marry early. They are fond of dancing and going to fairs, and make no regular amusement, cards and cock-fighting being held as disgraceful."

Be that as it may, there was some frailty of the flesh. There are reports that certain guides to the nearby Giant's Causeway were less than helpful, and when they did earn money it was soon spent dissolutely.

Despite the relative prosperity of the times, people were still seeking a fresh start elsewhere.

"About 40 persons (average) annually migrate to America. Chiefly to the British settlements. September is the usual time for embarking. From 60 to 70 persons annually go to the English and Scottish harvest and return when they are over."[12]

"Hugh McGahie and his donkey and cart outside a thatched house at Bushmills" — this was taken by Robert John Welch, the doyen of early Ulster photographers. Born in Strabane in 1859, he later moved to Belfast and for over half-a-century he built up an outstanding reputation with his work on a wide variety of subjects. He died in 1936.

This picture of Bushmills showing the Bridge End Bar and the sign for "Old Bushmills" dates from the second half of the 19th Century. The angler in the foreground is a reminder of the excellence of the Bush as a fishing river. It is worth noting that the water-wheel on the far side of the bridge is in good condition.

This late 19th Century picture by Robert Welch is of the Causeway Tram, Europe's first hydro-electric tramway which appeared in 1883 and remained operative until 1950. It inspired many stories and verses, including this from Hugh Speers' ballad "The Giant's Causeway Tram";

"Oul' Lurcher Tom McConaghy was spitting on the floor
Till a certain lady passenger could stand the sight no more
She asked conductor Charlie Shaw if spittin' he'd permit
And sez he 'Aye surely missus, just you go ahead and spit!'"

Bassett also reveals that the River Bush drives two corn mills and a scutch mill "and it is also utilized in generating motive power for the electric tramway, running between Portrush, Bushmills and the Giant's Causeway[16]".

Advertisements

The "Book of Antrim" carries advertisements for local businessmen, including Lyle Taggart — "general merchant" and Daniel Taggart, "auctioneer and valuator". There are adverts for no less than three hotels. E. C. Suckling, proprietor of his "Commercial and Family Hotel" offered room and board, and a drive to the sea every morning for a mere 30/- a week. There were positively NO EXTRAS. This service was for those who came to Portballintrae for bathing, but anglers who wished to fish the Bush could have rooms and board for 25/-. Presumably the extra five shillings a week went on transport, and the hotel offered "Good stabling and posting cars."

Hugh McDowell in his "Commercial Hotel" offered much the same services to anglers, tourists and excursionists "from Belfast and elsewhere to the Giant's Causeway". However he was coy enough not to mention prices but gave the assurance that there were "Moderate charges in every department". D. McIlroy in his "Family and Commercial Hotel" offered almost identical services, but his charges — unspecified — were "strictly moderate".

Most important, each in their own way underlined that Bushmills enjoyed a brisk tourist trade due to its proximity to the good salmon and trout fishing, sea-bathing (which was then extremely popular) at Portballintrae, and inevitably the Giant's Causeway which was indeed believed to be one of the wonders of the world.

Distinguished

One distinguished visitor to the Giant's Causeway was His Royal Highness Arthur William Patrick Albert, the third and favourite son of Queen Victoria. He was created Duke of Connaught and Strathearn in 1874. Prince Arthur went to the Causeway in April, 1869 and the contemporary Coleraine Chronicle newspaper states;

"The Prince journeyed by special train from Derry, via Coleraine to Portrush. The passing of the Royal train over the Bann at the railway bridge near Coleraine was signalled by a salute fired by direction of Mr. Stewart Hunter, chairman of the Town Commissioners, from the cannon placed specially for the occasion in the Anderson Park. This had been captured 'by the valour of Irish and other soldiers from the enemies of England in the wars of the Crimea' and was presented to the town by Lord Naas. On the arrival of His Royal Highness at Portrush, the Royal visitor proceeded to the Antrim Arms Hotel (later the Northern Counties). His Royal Highness made the journey to the Causeway, via Bushmills, in a carriage provided by Sir Edmund Macnaghten. There was then no electric tram; it was not introduced until fourteen years later. At the Causeway the Prince viewed the various items of interest and paid a visit to the famous caves to which he was rowed in a boat manned by gaudily-dressed fishermen. (They were in blue and white jerseys to represent the waves of the sea.)

The Prince on his return to Bushmills from the Causeway fished the Bush for an hour. "But no angler, however skillful" (according to the "Chronicle" of the day) "could from a stream, no matter how richly stocked, lure a fish when honoured or bothered with a following like that which accompanied the Royal angler on that occasion."

Many years later, in 1935, Mr. H. A. Boyd of Ballycastle sent a copy of the "Coleraine Chronicle" to the Equerry to His Royal Highness as a reminder of the

Further glimpses of life near Bushmills at the turn of the century are provided by a series of letters by Helen Macnaghten, a sculptress and the great grand-daughter of the Sir Francis Workman Macnaghten who had done so much to develop Bushmills. Helen Macnaghten's letters show a lively interest in the Gaelic League, the Boer War, the state of the churches, and the Suffragette Movement, as well as the Bushmills of her day. In a letter dated about 1910 she tells her friend Anne W. Richardson, a Bessbrook lady studying at Westfield College in London, about a forthcoming hurling match ". . . everyone has promised to try and keep their tempers in which I hope they will succeed, but feeling about games runs very high here, last Saturday a Bushmills football player struck the referee because he did not like his decision . . ."[20] Some things do not change!

World Affairs

Helen Macnaghten had firm opinions about world affairs. "I am glad that I do not require foreign (especially Belgian) testimony as to the superiority of an

Runkerry House — built in 1883, this was the home of sculptress Helen Macnaghten, a great grand-daughter of Sir Francis Workman Macnaghten who did a great deal to develop Bushmills. Helen Macnaghten's letters to a friend in the early part of this century provide a lively commentary not only on Bushmills but on world affairs. The house is now used as a training centre in outdoor pursuits for young people.

Englishman to a Boer . . . someone was telling me today that Kitchener is too lenient and will not carry out his proclamation and is thereby prolonging the war . . ."[21]

She also describes a visit to Egypt, and expresses doubts about the work done by the American Mission . . . "it does not seem quite fair or wise to treat the Copts like heathens and turn them into Presbyterians."[22] She expresses her admiration for Islam and gives her opinion that attempts to convert Mohammedans to Christianity was a futile and dangerous undertaking.[23]

She also writes about temperance, and non-temperance. "I fancy some of the Temperance extremists hardly know what they are doing. Mr. Barclay was also telling me a great deal about Denmark, they have solved the drink question there without any confiscation. The Temperance people agreed that beer with under 2¼ per cent of alcohol should be considered a Temperance drink, the brewers produced such a beer, and the government helped by making the duty very low for that and raising it for anything beyond, he says Denmark far from being the most drunken country in Europe is practically sober . . ."[24] She writes in another letter "we are hoping to do something for Irish on Rathlin this winter . . . It will be a great struggle I fear with the bigoted party in the Church of Rome, the best priests are on the League side. A new Orange Lodge was founded near here last week, a violent speech from Mr. Moore and then much drunkenness . . .[25]"

Such views from an independently-minded young woman at the beginning of the 20th century provide a fascinating insight on an age when Bushmills and the Middle East were literally a world apart. But as the century wore on the world became engulfed in major wars, and the sacrifice and service of Bushmills people are symbolised in an imposing War Memorial in the town's main square. This is the figure of a bronze soldier on a granite plinth.

Modern Bushmills is a neat, prosperous looking town. The clock tower in the picture is an imitation Irish round tower erected by the local landlord Sir Francis Macnaghten in 1874. In the centre of the Square is the War Memorial — a bronze soldier on a granite plinth by C. L. Hartwell, A.R.A.

Distilling had taken place in Ireland long before "Old Bushmills" was granted its licence in 1608. There are many references to "Usquebagh", "Uisce Beatha" and "Aqua vitae", the "water of life." Several sources mention "aqua vitae" in the 13th century and they claim that in 1276 Sir Robert Savage, ground landlord of Bushmills, suitably fortified his troops before battle.

CHAPTER THREE

"1608 And All That"

The origins of whiskey in Ireland are wreathed in rhetoric. There are few enough factual milestones to guide the traveller through the swirling mists of Celtic history. But Irish rhetoric has a charm of its own.

It is known that distilling had taken place in Ireland long before *Old Bushmills* was granted its licence in 1608. In previous centuries there are references to "Usquebagh", "Uisce Beatha" and "Aqua vitae", the "water of life." Samuel Morewood in his celebrated "History of Inebriating Liquors", published in 1838, claims that "aqua vitae" was first known in Europe in the reign of Henry II (1133-89). He claimed further that "spirituous liquors" had been noticed in some of the earliest songs and writings ". . the English, shortly after the invasion, in the time of Henry II, found the people indulging in potations of this liquour. . . it is more than probable that it was known in Ireland before the English were acquainted with it."[1]

Several sources mention "aqua vitae" in the 13th century. They claim that in 1276 Sir Robert Savage, ground landlord of Bushmills, suitably fortified his troops before battle. The story, taken from the "Annals of the Savages" is contained in a booklet published by the *Old Bushmills* Distillery Co. Ltd. in 1938.

"Sir Robert Savage having prepared an army against the Irish, allowed to every soldier, before he buckled with the enemy, a mighty draught of aqua vitae, and killed, for provision on their return, beef, venison and fowl in great plenty; which divers of his captains misliked, and considering the success to be uncertain, esteemed it better policy to poison the cates and do them away, than to cherish a sort of caitiffs with princely food, if aught should happen to themselves in this adventure of so few against so many. Hereat smiled the gentleman and said 'Tush, ye be too full of envy. This world is but an inn, whereunto ye have no special interest but are only tenants at the will of the Lord. If it please Him to command us from it, as it were from our lodging, and to set other good fellows in our room, what hurt shall it be to us to leave them some meat for their suppers, let them hardly win it and wear it. If they enter our dwellings, good manners would no less than welcome them with such fare as the country breedeth and with all my heart much good may it do them. Notwithstanding I presume so far upon your noble courage that verily my mind giveth me that we shall return at night and banquet ourselves with our own store."[2]

Different

Interestingly, Morewood seems to refer to the same story, though he gives it a different date. "It would seem that aqua vitae was employed in Ireland, at one time, as opium has been amongst the Turks, to inspire heroism; and this is exemplified in the case of a knight, named Savage, that lived in 1350, who, previously to entering the field of battle, ordered to each soldier a mighty draught of aqua vitae."

In the Book of Leinster there is the story about a feast at Dundabheann, near Bushmills. Some of the guests imbibed the local distillation so freely that on leaving at midnight they started out for Louth on the East Coast but eventually arrived at Kerry in the South-west!

Some writers believed that the secret of distillation came from India. Others pointed to the Middle East, where Christian missionaries discovered the Arabs distilling aromatics in an alembic. Yet others thought that the secret had originated in Europe. Samuel Morewood distils entertainment out of speculation, in almost equal proportions.

"The strong affinity between the Irish language and the primitive languages of Asia, as stated by Vallancey and other etymologists, and the intercourse the Irish had with that quarter of the world, lead to the supposition that the art of distillation was introduced directly from India; but it is more than likely that it was received from Spain or Italy where it was early known under the epithet of acqua vite or acqua di vite (water of the vine), the grape being the material from which a spirit was originally extracted in those countries.

"The monasteries being the repositories of science and the original dispensaries of medicine, it is a natural surmise that the term acqua vite was there corrupted into the Latin and universal appellation Aqua vitae (water of life), from its salutary and beneficial effects as a medicine; and from the Latin tongue being the general conveyancer of scientific discovery, as well as of familiar correspondence, the term aqua vitae may have crept into common use to signify an indefinite distilled spirit, in contradistinction to acqua vite, the mere extract of the grape."

"The dissolution of the monasteries gave the secret of this invention to the public, and the elixir of the alembic soon attained the summit of popular regard."[3]

Definition

Dr. Samuel Johnson, the same who had declined to visit the Giant's Causeway, produced in 1755 his famous Dictionary which maintained its prominence in England for nearly a century. The good Dr. Johnson defined "usquebaugh" thus; "(An Irish and Erse word which signifies the water of life.) It is a compounded distilled spirit, being drawn on aromaticks; and the Irish sort is particularly distinguished for its pleasant and mild flavour. The Highland sort is somewhat hotter; and, by corruption, in Scottish they call it whisky."

Whatever were the doubts about the exact origin of whiskey, there was certainty about the benefits of such a "medicinal compound." Morewood again;

"Aqua vitae was first used in the country as a medicine, considered as a panacea for all disorders, and the physicians recommended it to patients indiscriminately for preserving health, dissipating humours, strengthening the heart, curing colic, dropsy, palsy, quartan fever, stone, and even prolonging existence itself beyond the common limits".[4] (It is interesting to note that today many physicians claim that alcohol in moderation can be beneficial to health, including certain cardiac conditions.)

But for some people of all ages it has been more than that. Morewood writes of the 16th century.

"Notwithstanding the frequent use of spirits at that period, our wealthy and luxurious countrymen indulged in the use of rich and costly wines. Hollinshed, in his Chronicles, says that the great Shane O'Neill, who proved so violent an opponent to Elizabeth, usually kept in his cellar at Dundrum, 200 tuns of wine, of which, as well as usquebaugh, he drank copiously, and sometimes to such excess, that his attendants were often obliged to bury him in the earth, chin-deep, until the heating effects of the intoxication had abated."

Some people imbibed too well, rather than wisely! "Hollinshed in his Chronicles says that the great Shane O'Neill, who proved so violent an opponent to Elizabeth, usually kept in his cellar at Dundrum, 200 tuns of wine, of which, as well as usquebaugh, he drank copiously, and sometimes to such excess, that his attendants were often obliged to bury him in the earth, chin-deep, until the heating effects of the intoxication had abated."

Difficulties

In his book "Irish Whiskey", E. B. McGuire illustrates the difficulties in tracing the precise history of individual distilleries during these years, though there is no doubt that a great deal of distilling — legal and illegal — took place. He writes; "In the north and north west of Ireland there was such an impact from illicit distillers that it becomes impossible to trace the fortunes of either distillers or distilleries until the nineteenth century was well advanced. From about 1780 many licensed distillers ceased or turned to illicit manufacture. Occasionally a new licensed distillery might appear as the result of laws designed to attempt illicit distillers to mend their ways; or a determined man might persist in legal manufacture with periods when his still was silent and, therefore, was not shown in official returns.

"In the last case it did not necessarily follow that there was no distilling, it meant that there was no legal distilling. The distillery at Bushmills is an example. It is claimed that the present distillery was founded in 1743 for illicit distilling and that it became a legitimate distillery in 1784. In 1782 there were five licensed distilleries in Bushmills with stills in the range 200 to 252 gallons. Official returns of distillers do not show any distiller in Bushmills in the following years until 1833. This does not mean that no distillery existed during these years. Circumstances were so abnormal because of the extent of illicit distilling that any legal distillery would have great difficulty in marketing a regular production. It is probable that at least one distillery was maintained, but was silent for long periods and these may have coincided with the times of the official returns.

"Perhaps there was a little illegal manufacture as a sideline to keep alive. Bushmills malt whiskey had a good reputation in the early nineteenth century which supports the view that a distillery did operate from time to time, and there might have been a few unofficial runs through the still. Nevertheless the information is too meagre to trace which one of the five distilleries in 1782 survived into the next century or who owned it."[17]

The illicit distilling, mentioned by McGuire, is one of the main features of the story of whiskey and poteen until the later part of the 19th century. Illicit distilling continues today on a much reduced scale, as witnessed by the occasional court case in the local newspapers. (This writer's limited experience of poteen was confined literally to a taste in South Armagh near the border. The owner of the house, at that time a well-known figure, explained gravely that in the event of any enquiries from the police he kept the liquid strictly as a liniment for his ailing knee!)

Illicit

Mrs. Julia Mullin in her "Causeway Coast" traces neatly one human dimension to illicit distilling. "Although only those holding licences were legally allowed to distill, illicit drink or poteen has been made down the centuries in Ireland. Those licensed to make whiskey could not produce sufficient quantities to satisfy demand in a country where little beer was made, but as well as this, this 'parliament' whiskey was considered by many to be much inferior to poteen, which not only was thought

The distilling of illicit spirit or "poteen" increased greatly when duties were imposed on spirits in the 17th century. The practice was widespread until the late 18th century. There was a turning point in 1823 when the method of charging duty was changed, and illicit distilling degenerated into a small-time supply to a local market of customers who could not afford to buy legal whiskey. Illicit distilling continues today but on a very limited scale. These pictures by Robert Welch show children "guarding" a poteen still in Connemara, and a group of tourists, also in the West of Ireland, taking a much closer look! Both pictures date from around the 1890's.

to taste better, but was said to be purer and less harmful. However, perhaps the main reason for illegal distilling was the poverty of the peasants, many of whom found poteen-making their only chance to make ends meet and pay the high rents charged by the landlords. Also, again because of their poverty, they couldn't afford to pay the price of 'parliamentary' whiskey, and as they were not notably law-abiding, they were very willing to try their hand at illicit distilling."

She notes that although there had been private stills around Bushmills for many years, there was a sudden increase at the end of the 18th century and in the early 19th, due to greater taxation imposed by the Government.

"Mr. George Atkinson Wray, then living at Clogher (Bushmills) wrote in 1815; 'Private stills, they have all at once risen up here and to a degree that would astonish you, it is computed that there are not less than 40 stills in the Baronies of Cary and Dunluce, you will imagine what a destruction such as system as that would make in the conduct and morals of the people if it gets leave to continue much longer the whole country will shortly be a scene of idlings and intoxications to which every other outrage or villanry would soon succeed.' "

She quotes another letter written in 1834 by Horatio Roberts of Dervock "whose job was to track down stills." He tells of going out about 3 a.m. or 4 a.m. to "fall upon" the stills about daybreak. And in the letter to his mother he relates that he has been tolerably successful in his searches and that the Collector of Taxes in Coleraine has a good opinion of his work. Another story about poteen points to heartbreak for a local minister. "Not far away, Portstewart did a thriving trade in poteen in the early 19th century, but in this case the poteen was not made locally, but brought across from Inishowen in small boats. Here also tobacco was landed illegally from vessels passing on into the channel. And Ballycastle, though rather far away from the poteen producing centres had a port where shipping calling in connection with the collieries afforded excellent opportunities for the export of poteen.

"In 1824 the government was urged to station customs officials nearby. Here also tobacco smuggling was carried on, and officials were urged to be on the alert for tobacco being brought in from America. At this time Hugh Hill, the only son of Rev. Charles Hill, vicar of Ramoan, was the recognised head of the smugglers in the district and captain of a lugger which smuggled out poteen brewed in the Glens of Antrim and brought back from Scotland cargoes of tobacco and other contraband. His vessel was captured by the revenue cutter when at anchor in Ballycastle Bay, and Hill and his crew sentenced to transportation."[18]

Skullduggery

Tales of skullduggery and violence were plentiful, in the manufacture and detection of illicit spirits. Samuel Morewood, in the elongated yet dignified prose of the early 19th century, tells the sad story of two revenue officers who were literally spirited away.

"On the approach of the Assizes in 1803, when many were about to be prosecuted for illicitly distilling, an officer, stationed at Dunfanaghy, in the County of Donegal, who was to support the informations, was suddenly seized, blind-folded,

Portstewart did a thriving trade in poteen in the early 19th century. The illicit spirit was not made locally, but brought across the sea from Donegal in small boats. This photograph of Portstewart, in the late 19th century, showed the site of the first harbour. Portstewart today has a fine harbour and promenade, and a reputation far removed from that of a "poteen" centre!

and carried away by a body of men in disguise, and brought to the island of Arran on the western coast. From thence he was conveyed to the islands of Goal, Innismay, etc., where he was closely confined, often threatened with the loss of life, and was even obliged, by way of humiliation for his active services, to assist in the working of an illicit still; while, like another Tantalus, the cup of pleasure was held to his parched lips, without the liberty of gratifying his thirsty desires. At the end of thirteen days, when the necessity for his confinement had ceased, he was again blindfolded, taken from the island, and sent a considerable distance into the interior of the country, where the mask was removed from his face, and he was allowed in the solitude of night, to make his way to his disconsolate family, who, all the time, had looked upon his restoration as hopeless."

"Another officer, on a similar occasion, was hurried from his bed, without any covering except his shirt and trousers, put into a sack, thrown across the back of a horse, and, in this manner, was conducted to the margin of a lake, where, in his own hearing, a consultation was held whether he should be drowned by tieing a stone to the sack and committing it to the deep, or that he should be put to a more lingering and torturing death. In this awful state of suspense he was removed to a mountainous part of the country, where he was subjected to every kind of insult and privation, continually menaced with death in every shape of barbarity, led out at night as if to be executed, and again conducted to his solitary habitation, anticipating a renewal of further cruelties.

"In this state he was retained for a considerable time, till the Judge who presided at the Assizes, during the trial of some persons for illicitly distilling, suspecting the

Tales of skullduggery and violence were plentiful in the manufacture and detection of illicit spirits. Samuel Morewood in a book published in 1838 tells of a law-enforcement officer who had evidence implicating many people who were to be tried at the Donegal Assizes in 1803. He was "suddenly seized, blind-folded" and transported to lonely islands where he was kept for nearly two weeks until "the necessity for his confinement had ceased." The threat of an extra sentence on the accused, if found guilty, often had the salutary effect of persuading the accomplices to release the prisoner.

parties as being accessary to this outrage, told them, that if the officer who had been taken away, were not immediately liberated, he would pass such a sentence on them as would for ever put it out of their power to commit such another offence, and gave them but twenty-four hours for his restoration. This had the desired effect: the unfortunate man was again put into a sack and restored to his family in the same manner as that in which he had been carried away."[19]

Struggle

The struggle between the authorities and the illicit distillers is related in detail by McGuire in his "Irish Whiskey." His summary of those years is more than adequate:

"Looking back over the history of illicit distilling it is clear that it emerged from domestic distilling when duties on spirits were imposed in the seventeenth century and that such distilling was widespread in most parts of the country till the late eighteenth century. After 1780 there was a fairly rapid change in this picture owing to the introduction of the still licence charge on legal stills and a steady increase in the number of these charges.

"In the northwest and west the small legal stills were displaced by the illicit distiller and in the rest of the country there was severe competition between the legal distiller evading the duty and the illicit distiller, with the former generally winning. Nevertheless in the whole of Ireland at this time large quantities were coming from illicit stills and they were a real threat to the legitimate industry as well as the revenue. There was a turning point in 1823 when the method of charging duty was changed though it is very doubtful if this was realised at the time. Licensed distillers could use better apparatus and increase the size of their operations. Their produce too was greatly improved and their working much more economical.

Licensed distilleries were established in notorious illicit distilling areas and competed successfully. Better methods for suppressing the private still were evolved, the revenue police strengthened and reorganised, and the illicit distiller driven into remote areas where he was harrassed first by the revenue police and later by the constabulary. The illicit distiller degenerated into a small-time distiller with a strictly local market generally of persons who could not afford to buy legal whiskey. In the latter half of the nineteenth century any threat to the distilling industry from illicit distillers had disappeared. Detections were, for the most part, trivial cases of no more consequence than poaching. So far as the distilling industry was concerned, illicit distilling could be ignored. The industry's main competitors were, as fundamentally they had always been, the spirit importer and the brewer."[20]

References

1. History of Inebriating Liquors by Samuel Morewood, published 1838 by William Curry, Jun. and Company, and William Carson. Longman, Orme, Brown, Green and Longmans, London.
   Fraser and Company, Edinburgh. Page 615. (The full title of this work is worth recording in itself; "A Philosophical and Statistical History of the Inventions and Customs of Ancient and Modern Nations in the manufacture and use of INEBRIATING LIQUORS with the Present Practice of Distillation in all its Varieties; together with an extensive illustration of the Consumption and Effects of Opium, and other stimulants used in the East, as substitutes for Wine and Spirits.")
2. "Old Bushmills — being the story of Ireland's most famous whiskey and the district where it is made", published by the *Old Bushmills* Distillery Co. Ltd. Page 5-6. There is another reference to Sir Robert Savage in the Ulster Journal of Archaeology First Series 1858 Vol. VI, published by Archer and Sons, Belfast. It is contained in an article "On The Early Uses of Aqua Vitae in Ireland" which provides a fascinating background on the subject. The author quotes Campion "This Savage, having prepared an army against the Irish, allowed to every souldiour, before he buckled with the enemy, a mighty draught of Aqua Vitae, wine or old ale". Page 289.
3. History of Inebriating Liquors page 615.
4. Ibid. page 616. References to the medicinal virtues of Aqua Vitae are made in the article already referred to in the Ulster Journal of Archaeology First Series 1858 Vol. VI. The writer quotes Fynes Moryson's 'History of Ireland' — "And the said Humidity of Air and Land making the Fruits for Food more raw and moist; hereupon the Inhabitants and Strangers are troubled with Looseness of Body, the Country Disease. Yet for the Rawness they have an excellent Remedy, by their Aqua-Vitae, vulgarly called Usquebagh, which binds the Belly and drieth up Moisture more than our Aqua-Vitae, yet inflameth not so much." Page 289.
5. Ibid Page 618.
6. Ibid Page 619.
7. John Caillard Erck, A Repertory of the Inrolements of the Patent Rolls of Chancery in Ireland, Vol I, Part II pp 477-8.
8. Ibid Page 409. Erck is clear that the licence was granted to Taillor in the "fifth year" of the reign of James I who was proclaimed as successor to Elizabeth I when her death was announced formally in Dublin on April 5, 1603.
9. History of Inebriating Liquors pp 731-2.
10. "An Historical Account of the Plantation in Ulster 1608-1620" by the Reverend George Hill, published in 1877 by McCaw, Stevenson and Orr, Belfast, pp 393-4.

11. "An Historical Account of the Diocese of Down and Connor, Ancient and Modern" by the Reverend James O'Laverty, M.R.I.A., Fellow of the Royal Historical and Archaeological Association of Ireland. Parish Priest of Holywood. Vol. IV. Published in 1887 by James Duffy and Sons, 15, Wellington Quay, Dublin, and 1a Paternoster Row, London. Page 179.
12. Ibid Page 264.
13. Hill's "Plantation in Ulster." Page 393.
14. "The Siege of Derry" by Patrick Macrory published by Hodder and Stoughton Ltd. Page 71.
15. *Old Bushmills* booklet, published 1938. Page 7.
16. "The Whisky Distilleries of the United Kingdom" by Alfred Barnard, published first in 1887 by Harper's Weekly Gazette, and republished in 1969 by David and Charles Reprints, Newton Abbot, Devon. Page 432.
17. "Irish Whiskey — a History of Distilling in Ireland" — by E. B. McGuire published by Gill and Macmillan, Dublin and Barnes and Noble Books, New York, pp 382-3.
18. "The Causeway Coast" by Julia E. Mullin B.A., published in association with the *Old Bushmills* Distillery Co. Ltd. pp 133-4.
19. "History of Inebriating Liquors" by Samuel Morewood, pp 676-7.
20. "Irish Whiskey" by E. B. McGuire, pp 430-1.

CHAPTER FOUR

"*Blossoming Bush*"

References to *Old Bushmills* are sparse in the first part of the 19th century, though there is more documentary evidence in the later decades. There were several proprietors throughout the course of the century, but little is known about them — apart from the typically dry legal documents involved in various land deals and business ventures.

In "Irish Whiskey" there is a reference by E. B. McGuire to a James McKibben who paid duty on 10,216 proof gallons in 1833. McGuire notes that in 1835 there was only one Bushmills Distillery, but that there were two from 1840 to 1845 However, he also claims that the same James McKibben who paid duty in 1833 was still the owner in 1846, which points to some continuity of existence and ownership.[1] (In Slater's Directory of 1846, which is already quoted in Chapter Two, there is mention of "superior whiskey" produced from "the extensive distillery" of Mr. McKibben.)

For a period before 1855, the business was carried on by the Anderson family. On July 23, 1855 Robert Anderson leased the distilling concern to a Stewart Anderson for 21 years.[2] He included "the premises known as *Old Bushmills* distillery" but he reserved and excepted six dwelling-houses which are named, not inappropriately, "Aqua Vitae" Place! Stewart Anderson was to pay . . . "the yearly rent or sum of £100". This sum is evidence not only of the extent of the buildings but of the commercial attractiveness of the mid-19th century Distillery.

(Incidentally, the company's booklet published in 1938 claims that the first legalised Distillery was owned by a Hugh Anderson and that the townland on which the Distillery stands, Clogher-Anderson, is named after his family.[3] As far back as September 8, 1793, there was a Renewal Lease from Jean Mathews, Hugh Lecky and James White to the above-mentioned Hugh Anderson.)

Trot

The story is told locally of a member of the Anderson family who was known as "Lady" Anderson on the strength of having bred a winner of the Cheltenham Gold Cup. It was also said that her final wish was that her funeral procession would proceed at a good pace because this would be her last opportunity "for a trot"!

An extract from the manuscript of the valuation book 1859-60 gives the

Distillery's dimensions and the observation "This Distillery is not in working order at present but will be in a short time. The grain for malting is bruised by water power; diameter of water wheel 12.0 feet, fall of water about 4 feet."[4] The tenant is named as Thomas Millar, possibly as a nominee of the Andersons.

The Distillery remained in the hands of Stewart Anderson for only a short time and by August 20, 1860, he had sold his interest to James McColgan, a Ballymoney spirit merchant, and Patrick Corrigan for £500 cash. McColgan and Corrigan also undertook to execute the remaining 16 years of the 21 years lease from 1855 and to pay the rent of £100 per annum. Again this is evidence of the commercial viability of the concern.

Patrick Corrigan died in January 1865 and left his interest to his widow Ellen Jane who continued to run the business for 15 years with James McColgan. On November 26, 1880, it was bought by a number of businessmen who converted it into a limited liability company. McColgan and Corrigan sold the business for £3,000 and became directors in the new enterprise with 375 shares apiece. The shares were at £4 each, which gives a fair indication of their profits from 1865-1880.[5] The other directors were William Charles Mitchell, David Mitchell of Glasgow and William McColgan, a spirit merchant of Coleraine. Very few firms in Ireland became limited companies until after the First World War, so *Old Bushmills* was in the vanguard of this business development.

Fire

However one major event which had a significance above all others was the disastrous fire on November 25, 1885, which destroyed practically all the existing buildings. This fire is mentioned only in passing by sources for that period and it is also referred to briefly in a company Prospectus for 1896. But the details of that night in 1885 are recorded faithfully in the Coleraine Chronicle of Saturday, November 28th under the heading "Destructive Fire in Bushmills — The Distillery Destroyed."

"On Wednesday night the inhabitants of Bushmills and its neighbourhood were disturbed by the unwelcome cry of 'Fire', which was rung through the town shortly after eleven o'clock. No sooner than this cry was circulated than the inhabitants became alarmed and in proceeding in the direction in which the blaze was showing itself, the people thought, too truly, that the distillery was on fire. On proceeding to the South part of the town they found that the distillery, which is owned by a limited company in Belfast, was on fire.

"No sooner had the intelligence spread than every man and boy turned out, and on reaching the scene took hold of a bucket and carried water to the utmost of their endeavours in order to extinguish the flames, but this was all of no avail. The first part of the building which was observed to be ignited was the oil store and malt house. No sooner was this seen than Mr. Jas. Malcolm, Bushmills, proceeded to Sir F. Macnaghten's for fire extinguishers, but on this young man's arrival there he found that Mr. Luckland, the butler, had on observing the flames taken across the hills with the appliances but on his arrival the flames had reached to such an extent that they were found to be of no use whatever.

A disastrous fire on November 25, 1885 destroyed most of the "Old Bushmills" Distillery. A contemporary report relates that a Mr. Luckland, butler to the local landlord Sir Francis Macnaghten, had "on observing the flames taken across the hills with the appliances but on his arrival the flames had reached to such an extent that they were found to be of no use whatever."

Barnard also refers to the output of 100,000 gallons of whiskey "which is carted to the depot of the Electric Railway, which conveys it to the Portrush Railway Station and Harbour for delivery to all parts."[6]

He also notes, "The Company have lately erected very fine offices in Belfast, consisting of Board room, sampling room, secretary's and general offices." These are the Hill Street headquarters which figure so largely in the *Old Bushmills* story, from the mid-1880's.

During the early part of the decade it was known as "The Bushmills Old Distillery Co. Ltd.". In 1882 there was an exchange of letters about a trademark, with Bushmills being advised that there were certain similarities to other Irish trade marks in the matter of shamrock leaves. There was a reference also to a possible resemblance to the trade mark of the Dublin Whiskey Distillery Co. Ltd. But in the end the Bushmills Old Distillery motif appeared in the Trade Marks Journal of May 9, 1883. The applicant was William Stevenson Mitchell, company secretary, the description of goods was "Irish whisky" (sic.), the registration number was 29,942, the date of application was December 8, 1882, and the applicants gave due note that they had been in business "fifteen years before 13th August, 1875."[7]

This study of the "Old Bushmills" Distillery was taken by William Lawrence in the latter part of the 19th century. The tall chimney has since been demolished, and the general view of the Distillery has been changed by the distinctive Pagoda Towers — which here are conspicuous by their absence.

Courts

However, the story of Bushmills in these years is more than a history of transactions. As ever, the human stories bring flesh and blood to the bones of a company framework. There was big business, and little business too. The Coleraine Chronicle recorded the following details from Bushmills Petty Sessions on August 13, 1885.

"The 'Rale' Mountain Dew — Old John McKinlay, with whose face every visitor to the celebrated 'Giant's Well' at the Causeway must be familiar, was brought up by Constables McGuinness and Monahan and charged this time not for selling the water, but the real old Irish whiskey. Why John made such a terrible mistake at this time he could not answer, but by himself and his solicitor Mr. O'Rourke, he (John) admitted the offence and, as it was the second similar offence within 12 months their Worships finded him £2.10s,.plus costs."

Another court case of considerable interest took place in 1888 and was reported at length in The Northern Whig of December 15. Sir Francis E. Macnaghten, the local landlord, brought a prosecution against the Bushmills Old Distillery Company for allegedly having polluted a tributary of the River Bush "by allowing the 'wash' of the distillery to flow into it."

Samuel Dogherty, a waterkeeper employed by Sir Francis, gave evidence for the prosecution. He said that the water in the stream above the Distillery was pure, and

The Giant's Causeway became a fashionable tourist-centre, and visitors were a steady market for the local people trying to sell souvenirs and refreshments. Sometimes the liquid on offer was much stronger than the water in the "Giant's Well", and those found guilty of selling "the 'rale' Mountain Dew" risked arrest by the local constabulary. In August, 1885 "Old John McKinlay" was fined £2.10s plus costs at Bushmills Petty Sessions for such an offence.

This evidence settled the matter. The case was dismissed, and the business had taken so long that all other cases were adjourned to the next Court!

However, there was a sequel. On New Year's Day 1889 it was agreed that a John Young, a Thomas Sinclair "and a third person as shall be named by them" should determine whether any "reasonable and practicable" means could be devised for remedying the complaint "and what ought to be done by both parties under the circumstances." — a development foreshadowed in the court case. On May 20, 1899, Messrs. Young and Sinclair, together with a Sir Edward J. Harland, stated in a letter that they had listened to the parties concerned and "having personally visited the premises" were of the opinion that "the refuse matter from the Distillery now discharged into the stream passing the Distillery should be conveyed by piping to the sand hills or to the sea."

The cost would be £200 for a three inch pipe to the sand hills some 1½ miles away or £250 for a four inch pipe. "This expense we consider should be borne by the Distillery Company paying 70 p.c. and Sir Francis Macnaghten 30 p.c. The Distillery Company to maintain the pipes in good and efficient condition and Sir Francis Macnaghten to afford all reasonable facilities for the same. "Should the parties concerned elect to lay the pipes to the sea the additional expense to be borne by them in the same proportion as above." And so a potentially acrimonious matter was dealt with tactfully and with uncommon common sense.

Overseas

Though the story of Bushmills in those days could focus on a single but important court case near the very heart of the Distillery, that story also covered much of the world in an age of emigration, expansion and unbounded opportunities overseas. A steady volume of Irish emigrants had trickled and sometimes poured across the Atlantic and to many parts of the British Empire, bringing with them their taste for a native Irish product. And the Distilleries were quick to develop this market.

These were the years when *Old Bushmills* scored outstanding successes at international exhibitions. The Gold Medal and highest award for pure malt whiskey at the Cork Industrial Exhibition 1883; the gold medal at the Exposition D'Alimentation Et D'Economie Domestique in Paris 1886 and the only Gold at the Exposition Universelle in Paris 1889; the gold at the International Exhibition of Navigation, Travelling, Commerce and Manufactures in Liverpool 1886; the gold medal and first order of merit at the Adelaide Jubilee International Exhibition 1887; the gold at Chicago in 1893, gold at St. Louis in 1904, in London at the Franco-British Exhibition of 1908; and other awards down the years. A contemporary report gives an indication of the reaction in Bushmills to the good news from Cork. "The Bushmills Old Distillery Company through their manager, Mr. Lauder, brought their famed old Irish malt to the test of a public competitive examination at Cork exhibition a few days ago. On Saturday last, 22nd September, a telegram arrived here (at Bushmills) stating that the judges had awarded the Bushmills malt the gold medal. Thus has the Old Bush not only retained its prestige amongst distilleries, but it has taken its place in the front. The announcement on Saturday

During the later decades of the nineteenth century "Old Bushmills" won many awards for quality at Exhibitions in Britain, Europe and the United States. This picture is a copy of the Diploma won at the Franco-British Exhibition of 1908. It now hangs in the main office building of the Distillery. The repeated successes at Exhibitions generated great excitement. When news reached the town that "Old Bushmills" had won the gold medal at Cork in 1883; "it was the occasion of public rejoicing, tar barrels being burnt and the flute band promenading the streets."

evening in Bushmills was made the occasion of public rejoicing, tar barrels being burnt and the flute band promenading the streets."

That buoyancy was reflected back home. In 1887 the valuation records show that the valuation of the premises increased from £65 p.a. to £200 p.a.[8] In 1891 the company was re-formed and a capital of £200,000 was issued in equal proportions of ordinary and preference shares. The directors were Charles C. Connor, by then the Mayor of Belfast, and James S. Boyd — both of whom had been involved in the 1888 court case.[9] In a letter of June 10 the previous year to a Mr. Edmund McNeil JP, the writer noted that "Mr. Boyd and Mr. Connor are practically the owners of Bushmills Distillery." [10] The Prospectus for the 1891 formation of the Company noted "The business has for some time past been increasing very rapidly. It is in a most flourishing condition and the Directors confidently anticipate a continuance of prosperity. The sales within the last four years have almost trebled."

This Company, however, went into liquidation in 1895 and was re-formed in August 1896 with a share capital of £110,000 — 70,000 five per cent preference shares at £1 each and 40,000 ordinary shares at £1. The name of the Company was changed to "The *Old Bushmills* Distillery Co. Ltd.," and this was confirmed in writing by James Boyd on March 20, 1896. The Prospectus of August 24, 1896, provides a detailed description of the business.[11]

This famous sketch of the Shah of Persia being offered a bottle of "Old Bushmills" at an international exhibition in Paris now hangs in the Distillery's Potstill Bar.

The Subscription List will open on Monday, the 24th day of August, 1896, and close on or before Wednesday, the 26th day of August, 1896, for Town and Thursday, the 27th day of August for the Country.

THE

"Old Bushmills"

Distillery Company, Limited.

INCORPORATED UNDER THE COMPANIES ACTS 1862 TO 1890.

SHARE CAPITAL, £110,000.

70,000 Five per cent. Preference Shares of £1 each	£70,000
40,000 Ordinary Shares of £1 each	40,000
	£110,000

PREFERENCE SHARES.

Issue of £70,000 Five per cent. Preference Shares of £1 each.

The Preference Shares are entitled to a Preference Dividend of Five cent. per annum, and rank as regards Capital in priority to the Ordinary Shares.

ORDINARY SHARES.

Issue of £40,000 Ordinary Shares of £1 each.

DEBENTURES.

Issue of £70,000 Four-and-one-quarter per cent. First Mortgage Debentures of £100 each.

The Debentures are now offered for subscription at the price of 102 per cent.

The Debentures will be registered in the books of the Company, and the interest will be payable half-yearly on February 1st and August 1st.

The Debenture Stock and the Interest thereon will be secured by a First Mortgage to the Trustees for the Debenture Holders of the Freehold, Leasehold, and Copyhold Properties now purchased by the Company, and by a first floating charge (subject to a power reserved to charge further issues on hereditaments subsequently acquired), on all the other assets present and future of the Company.

The Debentures are redeemable at the option of the Company on the 31st December, 1906, at £105, upon giving six months' notice.

The Banks mentioned are authorised to receive subscriptions at the price of 102 per cent. for £70,000 Four-and-one-quarter per cent. First Mortgage Debentures, and at par for the above £70,000 Five per cent. Preference Shares and £40,000 Ordinary Shares.

PAYABLE:—

DEBENTURES.	PREFERENCE.	ORDINARY.
£ 5 per cent. on Application.	2/6 per Share on Application.	2/6 per Share on Application.
£47 per cent. (including premium) on Allotment.	7/6 per Share on Allotment.	7/6 per Share on Allotment.
£50 per cent. one month after allotment.	10/- per Share one month after allotment.	10/- per Share one month after allotment.
£102	£1	£1

Payment in full may be made on allotment, and as regards the Debenture Stock, under a discount of 2 per cent. per annum.

TRUSTEES FOR DEBENTURE HOLDERS.

JAMES DUFF, Barum House, Halifax, Chartered Accountant.
HUNTER MOORE, Solicitor, Newry.

DIRECTORS.

HON. HERBERT T. ALLSOPP,
Walton Bury, near Stafford, and Burton-on-Trent.

LORD TRIMLESTOWN,
Kew.

SAMUEL DUNCAN,
(Duncan, Alderdice & Co. Ltd.), "Old Distillery," Newry.

SIR EDWARD LEE,
14 Waterloo Place, London, S.W.

JOSEPH HETHERINGTON,
Wine and Spirit Broker, Liverpool.

The Vendor reserves the right to nominate two other Directors.

BROKERS.

DUBLIN.—D. D. BULGER, College Green and Stock Exchange.
MANCHESTER.—PIXTON & COPPOCK, 12, Half Moon Street and Stock Exchange.
LIVERPOOL.—HOOK & BRADSHAW, York Buildings, Sweeting Street and Stock Exchange.

BANKERS.

In ENGLAND.—THE UNION BANK OF MANCHESTER, LIMITED, Manchester or their London Agents, GLYN MILLS, CURRIE & CO., Lombard Street, E.C.
In IRELAND.—THE BELFAST BANKING COMPANY, LIMITED, Belfast
or any of their Branches.

SOLICITORS.

WALKER & ROWE, 8, Bucklersbury, London, E.C.

AUDITORS.

JOHN McCULLOUGH & CO., Chartered Accountants, Royal Avenue, Belfast.

REGISTERED OFFICES.

22 and 23 GREAT TOWER STREET, LONDON, E.C.

SECRETARY. (pro tem.)

MARTIN E. LYNAS.

The Company went into liquidation on a number of occasions in the later nineteenth and early twentieth centuries. In August 1896 it was re-formed with a share capital of £110,000. The Prospectus included a splendid picture of the Distillery which, after the fire of 1885, was "re-built in the most substantial manner." It was in 1896 also that the name changed from "The Bushmills Old Distillery Company" to the present title — The "Old Bushmills" Distillery Company Limited.

PROSPECTUS.

This Company has been formed to acquire the old-established Distillery business known as The "Old Bushmills" Distillery Company, Limited, situate at Bushmills, near the Giants Causeway, in the County of Antrim, Ireland.

The special make of Whisky manufactured at this Distillery under the Registered Title of "Old Bushmills" is of world-wide celebrity, and has been known for over 100 years. It has been supplied to the House of Lords, and amongst the numerous customers on the books of the Company are the Army and Navy Stores, London, the Civil Service Supply Association, Gordon Hotels, Hotel Cecil, Harrods Stores, and various Clubs, &c.

The Company takes over a large and valuable stock of Whisky, the greater portion of which is fully matured, dating back to the year 1885, and this asset is rapidly increasing in value owing to the scarcity of very old Whisky of fine quality.

The Distillery proper occupies a freehold site of about 6 acres, in addition to which there are about 16 acres of accommodation land and a farm of 19 acres held on lease. There is also an Office and Stores in Hill Street, Belfast; Stores in Market Place, Bushmills; Bonded Stores in Short Street and Albert Square, Belfast.

The Distillery was destroyed by fire in the year 1885 and was subsequently re-built in the most substantial manner and furnished with plant of the best and most modern description. Since the date named a considerable sum has been spent annually in maintaining and improving the buildings, machinery, &c., with the result that the concern is in thorough working order; moreover, the Distillery is so constructed that with a very small outlay its productive capacity can be doubled.

Upon the property there is a good manager's residence, also labourers' cottages, and ample stabling.

The storage accommodation is very extensive, and is capable of warehousing about one million gallons of Whisky.

Arrangements are being made for the sale of the Whisky throughout the United Kingdom, the Colonies and the United States, on a much more extended scale than hitherto, and already one very large North of England Brewery controlling about 300 houses has arranged to stock it.

The Distillery is situated in the centre of a large barley growing district, and ample supplies are available from farmers in the immediate neighbourhood.

The Company's own Maltings are capable of treating a large quantity during the season, and an extension in this direction must result in a considerable saving in the first cost of material.

There is a good local demand from farmers for grains at remunerative prices, and there is, upon the Distillery premises, a grains drying machine with all necessary working gear. This enables the price of wet grains to be kept up, and will prove a valuable source of income.

The importance of an adequate and suitable water supply is obvious, and in this respect the Distillery is particularly well situated, the Company having become some time since, by purchase, absolute owners of the entire water rights involved.

Referring to this point, Mr. Edmund Murphy, Chief Receiver Court of Chancery, and Government Arbitrator, who valued the prope... on behalf of the Company says:—"There is a never failing water supply of a quality that has rendered the Bushmills Whiskys famous."

In the brand "Old Bushmills," the Company acquires a very valuable property. The Whisky is well known not only in this country but in America, India, the Colonies, and the United States, having received the following awards:—Highest Awards, Cork, 1883, Liverpool, 1886, Adelaide, 1887; Diploma of Honor, Paris, 1886; Only Gold Medal, Paris, 1889; Silver Medal, Kimberley, 1892; and Medal at the World's Fair Exhibition, Chicago, 1894.

The Assets to be acquired by the Company consist of:—

	£	s.	d.
The Distillery and Property at Bushmills, which have been valued by Mr. Edmund Murphy, Government Arbitrator and Chief Receiver in the Court of Chancery, Dublin; ...	£20,003	6	1
Stores and Premises, Hill Street, Belfast, valued by Mr. T. A. Fisher, Property Broker, Belfast; ...	1,000	0	0
Plant, Machinery, Casks, and Implements, Vehicles, Live Stock, Chattels valued by Messrs. Hume & Gray, Valuators, Belfast; ...	16,258	12	6
Stock of Whisky, valued by Mr. W. W. Brydon, Spirit Broker, Trinity Square, London; ...	71,458	6	8
	£108,720	5	3
Book Debts (guaranteed by Vendor) ...	12,500	0	0
Duty paid on Whisky in Warehouse ...	2,200	0	0
Cash being proceeds of the present issue (in excess of the amount of purchase money) remaining available for additional Working Capital ...	25,000	0	0
Premium on Debenture Stock ...	1,400	0	0
	£149,820	5	3

In the above-named Assets no credit ... been taken for Goodwill.

The Company commences business free from all Liabilities and the Working Capital will be £112,558 6s. 8d., consisting of:—

		£	s.	d.
(A.)	**Stock of Whisky** ...	£71,458	6	8
(B.)	**Book Debts, (Guaranteed)** ...	12,500	0	0
(C.)	**Duty Paid on Whisky** ...	2,200	0	0
(D.)	**Additional Working Capital acquired by present issue**	25,000	0	0
		£111,158	6	8
(E.)	**Premium on Debenture Stock** ...	1,400	0	0
		£112,558	6	8

World-Wide

"The special make of Whisky manufactured at this Distillery under the Registered Title of "*Old Bushmills*" is of world-wide celebrity, and has been known for over 100 years. It has been supplied to the House of Lords, and amongst the numerous customers on the books of the Company are the Army and Navy Stores, London, the Civil Service Supply Association, Gordon Hotels, Hotel Cecil, Harrods Stores and various Clubs etc.; The Company takes over a large and valuable stock of Whisky, the greater portion of which is fully matured, dating back to the year 1885, and this asset is rapidly increasing in value owing to the scarcity of very old Whisky of fine quality.

"The Distillery proper occupies a freehold site of about 6 acres, in addition to which there are about 16 acres of accommodation land and a farm of 19 acres held on lease. There is also an Office and Stores in Hill Street, Belfast; Stores in Market Place, Bushmills; Bonded Stores in Short Street and Albert Square, Belfast.

"The Distillery was destroyed by fire in the year 1885, and was subsequently rebuilt in the most substantial manner and furnished with plant of the best and most modern description. Since the date named, a considerable sum has been spent annually in maintaining and improving the buildings, machinery etc., with the result that the concern is in thorough working order; moreover the Distillery is so constructed that with a very small outlay its productive capacity can be doubled."

"Upon the property there is a good manager's residence, also labourers' cottages, and ample stabling. The storage accommodation is very extensive, and is capable of warehousing about one million gallons of Whisky.

"Arrangements are being made for the sale of the Whisky throughout the United Kingdom, the Colonies and the United States, on a much more extended scale than hitherto, and already one very large North of England Brewery controlling about 300 houses has arranged to stock it."

The Company would commence business free of all liabilities and the working capital would be £112,558 6s. 8d. Not only was there a new company with a new name, but there was also a new board of directors. They were the Hon. Herbert T. Allsopp from Walton Bury, near Stafford; Lord Trimlestown of Kew; Sir Edward Lee of Waterloo Place in London; Joseph Hetherington, a wine and spirit broker from Liverpool; and the only local businessman, a Mr. Samuel Duncan, of the "Old Distillery" in Newry. However, the Vendor reserved the right to nominate two other Directors.

Prospering

The Company continued to prosper and in 1897 it announced a special bottling to mark the Diamond Jubilee of Queen Victoria. "In order to provide a real luxury for the celebration of the record reign of Her Most Gracious Majesty . . . we are bottling in Bond, under Government supervision, 10,000 Dozens of our Pure Old Malt Whiskey, distilled in the Jubilee Year of 1887." The price, by today's

Diamond Jubilee, 1897.

In order to provide a real luxury for the celebration of the record reign of Her Most Gracious Majesty,

Queen Victoria

we are bottling in Bond, under Government supervision,

10,000 Dozens

of our Pure Old Malt Whiskey, distilled in the

Jubilee Year of 1887.

Each Bottle will bear the official guarantee of age. This magnificent Old Whiskey may be obtained of all first-class Wine Merchants and Grocers throughout the United Kingdom.

Price 50/- per dozen; Nett Cash; Carriage Paid.

OLD BUSHMILLS DISTILLERY Co., LIMITED,

DISTILLERY, BUSHMILLS.

The Company flourished particularly around the turn of the last century, and in 1897 it announced a special bottling to mark the Diamond Jubilee of Queen Victoria "In order to provide a real luxury for the celebration of the record reign of Her Most Gracious Majesty."

standards, also gave cause for celebration — 50/- per Dozen: Nett Cash; Carriage Paid!

The price of spirits just before the First World War belongs to a different age. An Army and Navy Stores catalogue of 1913 quotes 48 shillings for 12 bottles of Bushmills Three Stars, Old Bourbon from America was 54 shillings, Very Old Liqueur Cognac was 165 shillings a dozen, and twelve-year-old Scotch was 48 shillings. Whiskey at 4/- a bottle seems, by modern standards, almost beyond belief.

Nearer home an invoice from *Old Bushmills* to Peter Fox of Gilford quotes two dozen pints of Old Malt Whiskey at 36 shillings a dozen, totalling £3-12-0. The case cost five shillings and carriage — by rail — was included. The date was December 27, 1916, when Europe was convulsed by war, and Ireland was in the midst of its struggle for independence. It was also the year of the Battle of the Somme when the flower of Ulster's youth, including men from Bushmills was crushed by the Kaiser's Germany on the muddy fields of Europe. There was another grim reminder of the war nearer home. In 1918 a German U-boat surfaced off Dunluce and shelled a passing steamer. In the Bayview Hotel in Portballintrae part of one of the shells is on display to this day with the inscription; "A portion of a shell fired from a German submarine which burst over this house on Sunday, May 6, 1918."

The story is told in detail by H. C. Lawlor in his book "Dunluce Castle and The Route" published by the Linenhall Press in 1919.

"Old Bushmills" survived and indeed thrived during the days of war. This picture which was taken in Falkirk, Scotland, shows veterans returning from the Boer War 1899-1902. Worth noting are the top hats and styles of the civilians, the uniforms of the soldiers, and the advertisement for "Old Bushmills" in the window of the local hostelry.

SPIRITS.

BRANDY.

All Proprietary Brands quoted are sold as described by the various shippers, and as received from them.

No.		Per doz. bots. Bots. incld.	:Per gal
*0.	Pale French Brandy (recommended for cooking	45/0	21/0
*1.	Pale Cognac ♔	55/0	26/0
*2.	Pale Old Cognac ♔ ♔	62/0	29/6
*3.	Pale Choice Old Cognac ♔ ♔ ♔	68/0	32/6
*5.	Brown Cognac	68/0	32/6
*6	Fine Liqueur, Old Cognac	80/0	—
*7	Very Fine Liqueur Cognac	104/0	—
*8	Very Fine Champagne Cognac, superior	127/0	—
*9	V.O.L. Very Old Liqueur Cognac	165/0	—
*10	N.P.U. Cognac, very Old and Choice	207/0	—

*These Brandies bottled by the Society are guaranteed Grape Spirit, and of Pot Still distillation.

	Per doz. bots. Bots. incld.
Denis Mounie ♧ ♧ ♧	69/0
Denis Mounie Grande Champagne Cognac, over 40 years old	186/0
Denis Mounie Fine Champagne Cognac, 1858	250/0
Raynal's, 1820, Very Finest Cognac, quite unique, over 80 years in cask	306/0
J. and F. Martell's *	63/0
" " * *	69/0
" " * * *	75/0
" " V.O.	86/0
" " V.S.O.	102/0
J. Hennessy's *	63/0
" * *	69/0
" * * *	75/0

	Per doz. bots Bots. incld.
Courvoisiers' "1 Diamond"	63/0
" "2 Diamonds"	69/0
" "3 Diamonds"	75/0
" "4 Diamonds"	77/0
Hine & Co., "Three Stars"	75/0
" "VSOP"	95/0
Exshaw's, No. 1	75/0
" No. 2	57/0
Australian (Joshua Bros.), "One Star"	50/0
" Irvine's "Three Stars"	60/0

SPANISH BRANDY.

(DOMECQ'S).

One Vine	60/0
Three "	70/0
Extra	86/0
Fundador, 1874	166/0

RUM.

No.		Per doz. bots.	:Per gal.
3.	Dark Jamaica (for cooking)	38/0	17/6
4.	White " "	40/0	18/6
1.	Old "	44/0	20/6
2.	Choice Jamaica, older	49/0	23/0
†5.	Very Fine, reputed to be over 100 years old	72/0	—

†Small quantity only.

WHISKY.

Scotch Malt and Grain Blend.

No.		Per doz. bots. Bots. incld.	:Per gal.
A.	Average age 9 years	44/0	20/6
B.	" 12 "	48/0	22/6

These Whiskies are added to the list to meet the demand for blends of Malt and Grain Whisky, and are recommended as being of good value.

The Scotch Whiskies quoted following this are made from Malt only, in a Pot Still, and all Irish Whiskies are Pot Still Distillation and properly matured. Special attention is called to the fine quality of the Society's own blends, also to the value given in strengths which are of a much higher degree than obtain in the majority of the proprietary brands, so extensively and expensively advertised.

Scotch.

No.		Per doz. bots. Bots. incld.	:Per. gal.
1.	Pure Malt, 4 years old	42/0	19/6
3.	" " fine, 6 years old	45/0	21/0
5.	Islay Malt	47/0	22/0
96.	Special Vat of fine Highland Malt makes, 13 years old	47/0	22/0
4.	Very fine pure Malt, 9 years old, special blend	49/0	23/0
14.	Coronation Whisky, a special blend of fine Malt makes, over 13 years old	50/0	23/6
15.	Talisker (Isle of Skye), 9 yrs. old	50/0	23/6
7.	Fine Old Vatted Highland Malt, from Glenlossie, Glenlivet Distillery, 10 years old	51/0	24/0
12.	Vatted Glendronach (Highland Malt), average age 10 years...	52/0	24/6
13.	Fine Old Vatted Glenlivet, average age 14 years	53/0	25/0
6.	Very fine, all Malt blend, 12 years old	54/0	25/6
8.	Liqueur, a choice old blend, pure Malt	57/0	27/0
†9.	Ben Nevis, 1880	80/0	—

Irish.

No.		Per doz bots. Bots. incld.	Per gal.
1.	Fine Old, Pot Still blend	44/0	20/6
2.	William Jameson, very old	46/0	21/6
9.	John Power & Sons, fine old	48/0	22/6
5	Bushmills (all Malt) Three Stars	48/0	—
*10.	**Army and Navy "Special"** a blend of fine old Pot Still Whiskies, average age over 10 years	49/0	23/0
4.	Jameson & Sons (a blend of old J. J. & S. Whiskies)	50/0	23/6
7.	H. S. Persse, very fine old	51/0	24/0
8	J. Jameson & Son's "Three Stars"	54/0	—
6.	Liqueur, J. Jameson & Sons	62/0	29/6

Canadian.

	Per doz. bots. bots. incld
Canadian Club (1905 make)	54/0

American.

Old Bourbon	54/0
Old Rye	60/0
"Hunter" Baltimore Rye	66/0

† Small stock only.

The above Whiskies, quoted in bulk, can be supplied in casks, containing 4, 7, and 14 gallons, which are recommended. Charge for cask, 4/0, 7/0, and 10/0 respectively. The same allowed if returned in good condition, carriage prepaid.

GIN AND HOLLANDS.

Gin.

No		Per doz. bots. Bots. incld	:Per gal.
1.	Unsweetened	35/0	16/0
2.	Sweetened	35/0	16/0
4.	Nicholson's Cordial	35/0	16/0
5.	" Dry	35/0	16/0
3.	Plymouth (Coates & Co.)	37/0	17/0
7.	Booth's Old Matured, dry (as supplied to the House of Lords)	42/0	—

Malt Gin.

		Per doz. bots. Bots. incld.
6	"Olma," Old Malt	42/0

Plymouth Gin.

Members residing in Devon and Cornwall, can be supplied with the above Gin direct from the Plymouth branch at 36/0 per doz. bottles, and 17/0 per gallon.

Hollands.

No.		Per doz. bots. Bots. incld.	Per doz. Cruchons
1.	De Kuyper's	40/0	—
*4.	**Very Fine and Old, the Army and Navy "Special"** (per gal. 17/6)	38/0	—
6a.	Boll and Dunlop, Old Liqueur, Schiedam, Red Label, in stone cruchons, reputed quart size	45/0	—
6.	Boll & Dunlop, Old Liqueur, Schiedam, Red Label, in stone cruchons, litre size	—	58/0
3.	Wijnand-Fockink's in stone flagons, litre size	—	62/0
5.	Bols' very old, in stone cruchons, $1\frac{1}{2}$ litres	—	68/0
5a.	" " " " reputed quart size	48/0	—

: Jars are charged for—1 gal., 1/6; 2 gal., 2/6. The same allowed when returned carriage prepaid.

Single bottles supplied at per dozen rate.

* Can only be obtained through the Society. The address cards must not be removed from returned cases, casks, and jars.

ARMY & NAVY STORES CATALOGUE 1913

The prices before the First World War belong to a different age. This catalogue from the Army and Navy Stores, London in 1913 lists 12 bottles of "Old Bushmills" Three Stars for 48 shillings, and 12 bottles of Old Bourbon from America cost only 54 shillings.

“In May 1918, a notable naval engagement took place between a German submarine and the merchant steamer “Wheatear,” off Dunluce Castle. The latter was on a voyage from Portrush to Cardiff, under the command of a Captain Davey, and had on board two naval gunners in charge of a 6-in. gun, mounted in the stern, and a crew of 15 men.

When the steamer had reached a point opposite Bushfoot, the German submarine, which was on the surface, about four miles to the north, opened fire upon it. The steamer turned, evidently to secure the shelter of the Skerries, firing rapidly at her adversary. When opposite Dunluce, she threw out a smoke-cloud, under cover of which she manoeuvred to avoid the shells from the submarine. A gentle south wind was blowing, which wafted the smoke-cloud towards the submarine, and in the cloud the steamer slowly approached the enemy, still firing. Careful aim on either side however was impossible, owing to the cloud; and as the

This plaque hanging in the hallway of the Bayview Hotel, Portballintrae, displays part of a shell fired over the building in May 1918 when a German U-boat surfaced off Dunluce and attacked a merchant steamer on its way from Portrush to Cardiff. The story is told in detail by H. C. Lawlor in his book “Dunluce Castle and The Route”, published in 1919.

contest at close quarters between the submarine and the heavily-laden merchantman would have been hopeless for the latter, she sought safety, when the smoke-cloud dispersed, behind the Skerries, eventually reaching Portrush Harbour in safety. She received a warm welcome from practically the whole population of the town and neighbourhood, who had assembled in thousands to greet her. On the berthing of the ship, the vast crowd sang the Doxology and "Rule Britannia." The brave captain and his crew were made honorary guests of the hospitable Northern Counties Hotel.

Shortly after the arrival of the steamer, a British airship arrived and pursued the submarine round the coast as far as off Larne, from whence came out a number of trawlers, by whom, it was reported, the submarine was captured or sunk.

In the engagement off Dunluce neither antagonist was hit, but several shells from the submarine fell in the village of Portballintrae, causing, however, little damage. During the action about 80 shots were fired; the weather was beautifully clear and the sea perfectly calm."

Profits

Despite the rigours of war, *Old Bushmills* prospered during these years. The price of whiskey increased and so did the profit margins on stocks that had cost a great deal less to produce. In that situation the maturing casks of *Old Bushmills* were literally liquid gold. The problem, however, was to avoid a Government windfall tax on such profits. The solution was liquidation. This was not to cease trading but to simply sell off an asset, in this case *Old Bushmills* whiskey.

According to the Wine Trade Review of February 15, 1921, a test case was brought by the liquidator to determine the rights of the preference shareholders to payment of dividends. The *Old Bushmills* Company Ltd. had been incorporated in August 1908 with a nominal capital of £110,000, divided into 70,000 preference shares and 40,000 ordinary shares. By a special resolution of August 5, 1920, the company was wound up and a liquidator appointed. By September 30, 1919, the undivided profits were £8,851 11s. 9d. and by the time of the winding-up itself, another £12,000 was available, leaving just over £20,000 in hand.

After satisfying the liabilities, there was a considerable surplus. The holders of preference shares were entitled to a preferential (non-cumulative) dividend of 5 p.c. They were not entitled to any other profits. In the event of winding-up, the assets (after the liabilities were accounted for) should re-pay the preference shareholders the amount paid on their shares. The remainder of the profits should go to other members of the company.

The previous dividend to preference shareholders had been made on March 31, some five months before the liquidation. Their lawyers argued that they were entitled to a share of the surplus earned between March 31 and August 5 — the date of liquidation. At the very least they were entitled to a dividend of the profits in that five-month period. However, the ordinary shareholders claimed that all the surplus assets belonged to them. And so it proved. Mr. Justice Astbury ruled that the preference shareholders had no claim in the winding-up, in respect of any dividend that had not been declared, and he made a declaration accordingly.[12]

Winding-Up

The winding-up also had repercussions with the Inland Revenue. "In Inland Revenue Commissioners v. *Old Bushmills* Distillery Co. Ltd., a company had carried on the business of whisky-distilling but went into liquidation, and the liquidator sold off the stock of whisky in parcels during a period of about two and a half years. He had stopped the manufacture of whisky after about seven months. He failed to sell the stock of whisky in bulk, and he made small purchases of spirit for blending and of bottles and casks, in order to facilitate sales of whisky in parcels. There was no other practical way of realising the whisky stocks. The proceeds of sales were regularly distributed among the creditors and the shareholders in proper priorities. It was held that the liquidator was merely realising the assets of the company and was not engaged in any trading operation."[13]

The case is outlined in detail in Edwards (Inspector of Taxes) v. *Old Bushmills* Distillery Co. Ltd.[14] The company was asked to pay Income Tax on the profit on whiskey sales made by the liquidator for the year ended April 5, 1921. On appeal the Special Commissioners upheld the assessment, but their decision was reversed by the Recorder of Belfast. He held that the sales by the liquidator were capital transactions carried out in the course of winding up the business. *Old Bushmills* were assessed the next year on similar transactions by the liquidator. The Company appealed, and the Special Commissioners discharged the assessment, because they felt themselves bound by the Recorder's decision for the previous year.

In turn the Crown appealed to the King's Bench Division of the High Court in Northern Ireland. The case was heard on December 10, 1924, and it went to the Northern Ireland Court of Appeal on January 27, 1925, and eventually all the way to the House of Lords. On February 7, 1926, their Lordships dismissed the Crown's appeal with costs. They held that the case must go back to the Commissioners to find out the facts, independently of the Recorder's decision for 1920-21, whether a trade had been carried on in 1921-22. The unusual feature about this case is that a Northern Ireland Company and its advisers had the courage to fight the Inland Revenue through the High Court and the Court of Appeal to the House of Lords. The long-term result was that the Government enacted legislation in 1938, just before the Second World War, to stop this legal loophole to tax avoidance.[15]

In plain man's terms, the Company had avoided paying tax. This was legal. They had not attempted tax evasion, which was and is illegal. Sir Thomas Phillips away back in the early 17th century had not been quite so successful in his dealings with the authorities. It was a long road from 1920 to 1608. In more ways than one, *Old Bushmills* had come of age.

Old Bushmills

IRISH WHISKEY

70° PROOF

DISTILLED 1920

Bottled and Guaranteed

by

FRED McNAIR

This poster advertises some of the last "Old Bushmills" distilled before the 1920 liquidation of the Company. This particular liquidation was a device to avoid a Goverment windfall tax on substantial profits made during the war. The "Old Bushmills" Distillery fought the Inland Revenue all the way to the House of Lords, and won its case. The long-term result was that the Government enacted legislation in 1938 to stop this legal loophole to tax avoidance.

References

1. "Irish Whiskey — a History of Distilling in Ireland" by E. B. McGuire, published by Gill and Macmillan, Dublin and Barnes and Noble Books, New York. pp. 383-4.
2. Public Record Office of Northern Ireland D 1326/31/17.
3. "Old Bushmills — being the story of Ireland's most famous whiskey and the district where it is made", published by the *Old Bushmills* Distillery Co. Ltd. pp. 8-9.
4 Public Record Office of Northern Ireland — Val 2B/I/26.
5. Public Record Office of Northern Ireland — D 1326/31/17.
6. "The Whisky Distilleries of the United Kingdom" published in 1887 by Harper's Weekly Gazette and re-issued in 1969 by David and Charles Reprints, Newton Abbot, Devon. Page 433.
7. Public Record Office of Northern Ireland — D 1326/31/43.
8. Public Record Office of Northern Ireland — Val 12 B/30/80.
9. Public Record Office of Northern Ireland — D 1326/31/17.
10. Public Record Office of Northern Ireland — D 1326/31/43.
11. Public Record Office of Northern Ireland — D 2610/CI/I.
12. Public Record Office of Northern Ireland — D 1978/10 Box IB.
13. Schedule D. Case I: Trading Income. BI.211, Part B1. Page 156. Also (1928) N.I. 56; 12T.C. 1148.
14. Edwards V *Old Bushmills* Distillery Co. Ltd. (In Liquidation) Tax Cases 10TC 285 and 5ATC 346. pp. 346-357.
15. "The History of the Taxation of Income — Simon's Taxes Vol. A p. 261 and also FA 1938, s 26, later ITA 1952, s 143, now TA 1970, s 137.

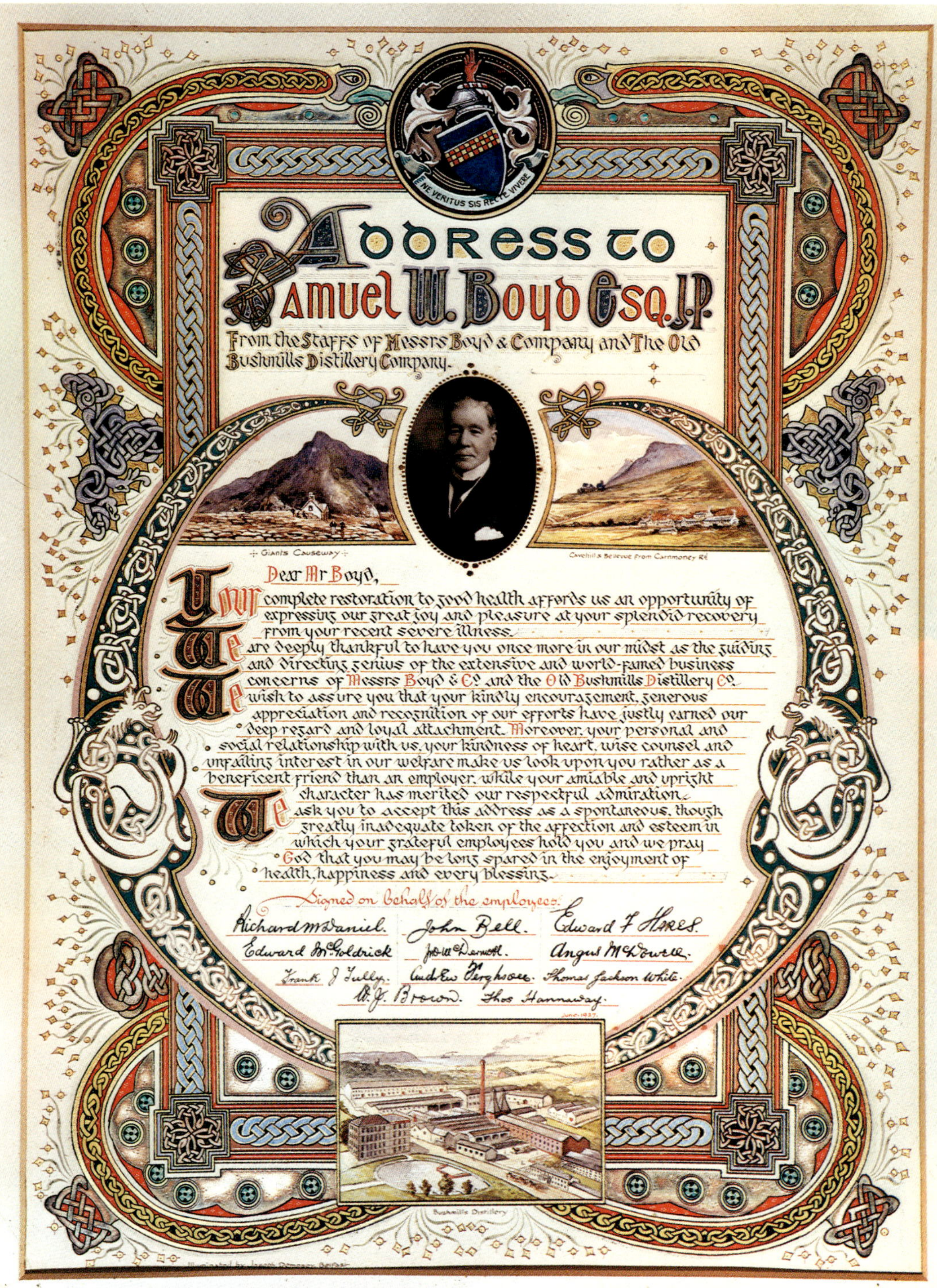

Address to Samuel W. Boyd Esq. J.P.

From the Staffs of Messrs Boyd & Company and The Old Bushmills Distillery Company.

Giants Causeway

Cavehill & Bellevue from Carnmoney Rd.

Dear Mr Boyd,

Your complete restoration to good health affords us an opportunity of expressing our great joy and pleasure at your splendid recovery from your recent severe illness.

We are deeply thankful to have you once more in our midst as the guiding and directing genius of the extensive and world-famed business concerns of Messrs Boyd & Co. and the Old Bushmills Distillery Co.

We wish to assure you that your kindly encouragement, generous appreciation and recognition of our efforts have justly earned our deep regard and loyal attachment. Moreover, your personal and social relationship with us, your kindness of heart, wise counsel and unfailing interest in our welfare make us look upon you rather as a beneficent friend than an employer, while your amiable and upright character has merited our respectful admiration.

We ask you to accept this address as a spontaneous, though greatly inadequate token of the affection and esteem in which your grateful employees hold you and we pray God that you may be long spared in the enjoyment of health, happiness and every blessing.

Signed on behalf of the employees.

Richard McDaniel. John Bell. Edward F Hares.
Edward McGoldrick [illegible] Angus McDowell.
Frank J Tully. [illegible] Thomas Jackson White.
W. J. Brown. Thos Hannaway.

June 1927.

Bushmills Distillery

The Illuminated Scroll presented to Samuel Wilson Boyd in 1927.

CHAPTER FIVE

A Family Affair

In June 1927 the employees of the *Old Bushmills* Distillery Company Ltd. and Messrs Boyd and Company presented an Illuminated Address to Samuel Wilson Boyd J.P.

This is a picture of an impression in oils of Samuel Wilson Boyd. He was a small man, "with a twinkle in his eye." He had his own inbuilt contradictions. He was a strict Presbyterian and, as a relation noted; "He would have been teetotal if it had not been for his business." He was a person of great integrity, and he possessed considerable business ability. He began his working life in licensed premises in Belfast and ended up by owning a Distillery.

Old posters and labels highlight a colourful history. Samuel Wilson Boyd, who bought "Old Bushmills" in the 1920's, also owned his own company which sold whiskey under the Boyd label.

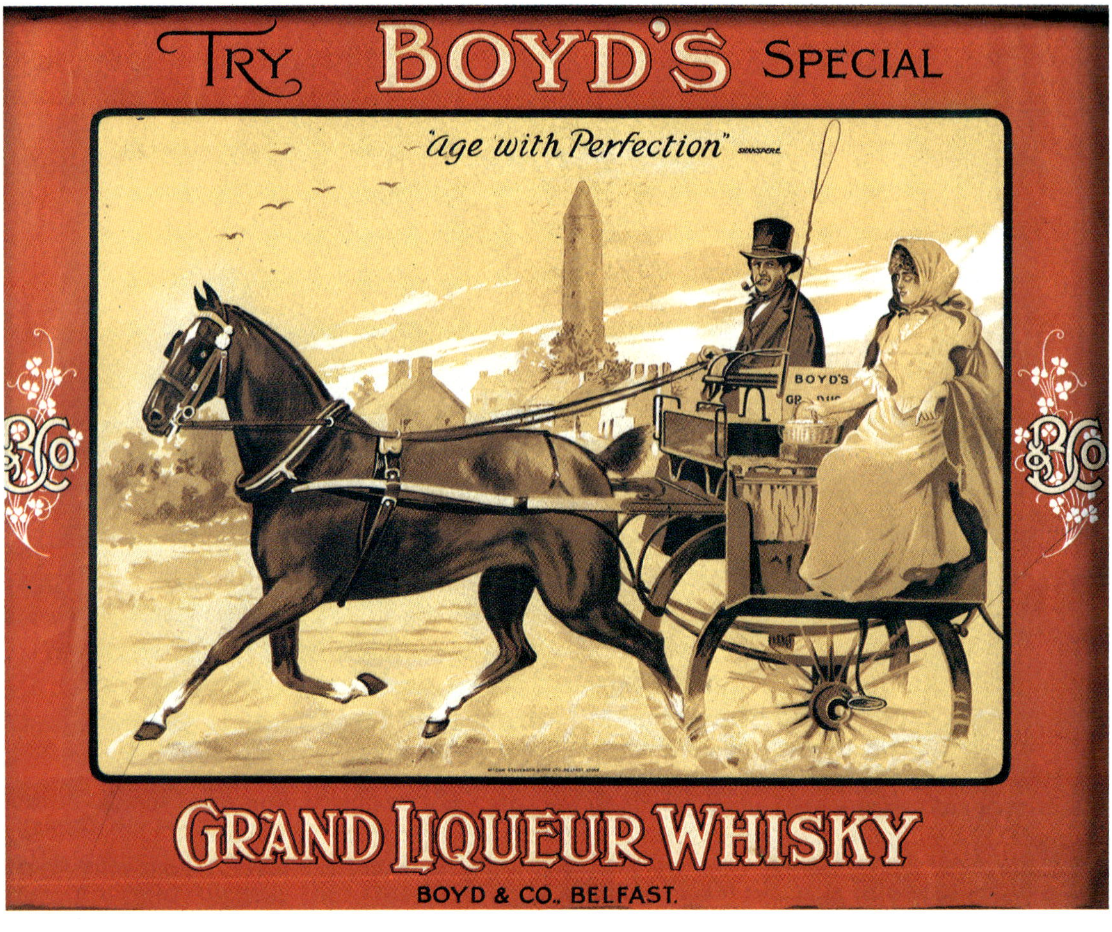

TRY BOYD'S SPECIAL

"age with Perfection" SHAKSPERE

GRAND LIQUEUR WHISKY

BOYD & CO., BELFAST.

Spirit Merchants" with offices in Hill Street and a customs and bonding store in Gordon Street. The invoice is for miscellaneous casks, assorted stocks, and office furniture, and it may well have been that Boyd bought out the Quin company and changed the name.

This company was separate from *Old Bushmills* right through the Twenties and Thirties until it was destroyed by the German air-raids on Belfast in 1941. The Boyd Company were wholesalers and they bottled and sold various products including brandy, rum, port, and sherry. In 1935 Wilson Boyd bought the stocks, trade marks and the goodwill of McConnell's Distillery, well known for its brand of "Old Cro' " whiskey. One of the advertisments showed, not suprisingly, a crow with the legend "Gives caws for delight!" Modern advertisers might note how a pun can be dreadful and memorable at the same time. . .

When the *Old Bushmills* Distillery came on the market in the early 1920's Boyd had the business and financial background to capitalise on such an opportunity. He bought the stocks and premises around 1923 and although it was not registered until April 3, 1930 as a limited company — some two years before his death — Samuel Wilson Boyd laid the foundation for a steady prosperity long after he died.

Loving

Physically he was short in stature, and some people likened him to a smaller version of David Lloyd George. Someone who knew him said "He was a small man, with a twinkle in his eye." He was a kindly and loving parent, though strict. He and his wife had fourteen children, though four died soon after birth. The survivors were Robert, Wilson, Clifford, Cecil, Austen and Herbert, who died at three. Wilson succeeded his father in the business in 1932. Austen was a director and he in turn succeeded Wilson as chairman and managing director in the mid-Sixties. There were also four girls in the family — Lillian, Marjorie, Olive and Hazel.

He was fond of writing to his children during his travels as a salesman. Two postcards to his then infant son Austen are carefully preserved. One was posted from Coagh, Co. Tyrone on February 18, 1904 and the other from Portaferry on October 16, 1908. In the first he relates what "the brothers of the little baby dog are saying to their mother" and in the second he expresses the hope that big brother Cecil Boyd is allowing baby Austen "to ride on his pony occasionally."

Austen's widow Mrs. Janet Boyd, an engaging and lively lady originally from Albany in New York State, has clear memories of her father-in-law.

"I was always predisposed to like him because he was my husband's father. I liked him and admired him, but I never really felt at ease with him. He was difficult to get close to. Although he was a pleasant man, and a very loving father, I don't think that his children got to know him. He always thought that he knew what was best for them. In that sense he was quite autocratic. They had little control over their lives." At his home on Belfast's Antrim Road he spent a great deal of his time in his favourite armchair. When he wanted people to come to him he simply pushed a bell on the wall. When younger members of the family were called in, they were rarely invited to sit down!

in Ulster are not like America, we do not have divorces here! I was dumbfounded — I'd just become engaged! The point was that we in America didn't think much of divorce either."

Samuel Wilson Boyd in many ways was an Ulsterman of his times — canny and conservative in equal proportions. Undoubtedly he was a well respected man, and like the head of most households, a little autocratic. Janet Boyd looks back on her parents-in-law with affection. "He was generous with his gifts, almost to the point of being lavish. When he returned from his last trip to America, he brought with him eight electric kitchen mixers. Seven were for his married children and one was for his own household. Indeed when he arrived at Moville with such a load, my husband had to take the trailer to meet the tender from the Anchor Liner."

"My father-in-law was a very astute businessman — absolutely upright, and a man of great integrity. My mother-in-law was patient, long-suffering and with a very loving nature. She never had an unkind thing to say about anyone. I loved her dearly." They were known to the entire family as "Pappa" and "Mamma", but throughout the firm there was only one "Mrs. Boyd." She had been a Miss Annie Magowan. The wives of the Boyd sons were known as Mrs. "Robert", Mrs. "Wilson", Mrs. "Clifford" and Mrs. "Austen."

Human

The history of a company can so often be the dry parade of details from dusty ledgers. But a company is run by human beings with their own passions, contradictions, ambitions, disappointments and hopes. Mrs. Janet Boyd is one of the few survivors of an age that will inevitably move beyond the scope of human memory.

Her finely-developed sense of history and her humanity are reminders that in the final analysis the story of a company is the story of people. History records that Samuel Wilson Boyd, the head of a company, died in 1932. He received a glowing obituary in the Belfast Newsletter of June 6 — alongside such heavenly and worldly matters as the reports on the Consecration of the then new Chapel of the Holy Spirit in Belfast Cathedral, and a court case in London where the daughter of Sir John and Lady Mullins swooned in the dock when charged with murder. Life went on, and the life of Samuel Wilson Boyd the businessman had been woven inextricably with the story of *Old Bushmills*. But there is room too for the memory of a kindly, if autocratic, father and of a human being who had to live like all of us with his own inbuilt contradictions.

Some of the atmosphere of the business and the dynamism of the Boyds is clearly evident from the newspaper and magazine cuttings of the period. In August 1927 "The Brewer" carried a detailed description of the Distillery, under the ownership of Samuel Wilson Boyd.

"The grain store is four storeys in height, the first two floors are laid in cement and used for malting. The third and fourth floors are used as grain stores, and have a capacity of 1,000 tons. All the latest machinery is fitted in the mill room and the mill is capable of grinding 300 bushels per hour. There are seven fermenting vessels with a capacity of 9,500 gallons each, and four copper pot stills. The five duty-free warehouses are built of stone and have a storage capacity of almost 1,000,000 gallons. Twenty acres of land are attached to the Distillery, which also comprises a manager's house, brewer's house, and workmens' cottages."

The article also contains a quote from the Editor of a London publication, "The New Era" — "Whilst we were looking through some of the letters we treasure, received from the departed friends of the 'happy days of long ago' we came across one from the journalist, Archibald Forbes, in which he thus referred to the famous '*Old Bushmills* liqueur whiskey'. 'It is time that the fair fame of real old Irish whiskey was vindicated; and as a means towards this end it should be understood that the *Old Bushmills* liqueur whiskey is manufactured by pot-stills only, and on comparing it with other spirits, I find none of them possesses the mellowness, generosity and wholesomeness of that famous whiskey'."

The Company was adept at advertising. Sporting fixtures and match programmes were particularly favoured. An advertisement in the Irish Association Football Guide for 1927-1928 (and the next year as well) stated "The International Favourite — After the Match try *Old Bushmills*. There were advertisements in country fair catalogues, the programmes for golf clubs, the catalogues for dog shows, police sports, provincial, regional and national newspapers and every form of communication to the public, including theatre bills. On August 31, 1929 there was a reference to the old Belfast Empire Theatre, which sadly has long since disappeared. There were programmes twice nightly — at 6.45 and 8.50. Admission was 2/4 and 1/6 to the Stalls, 1/3 to the Circle, and the Gallery cost sixpence.

Benefits

The advertising covered everything from the medicinal benefits of *Old Bushmills* — "The moderate use of a good whiskey, such as *Old Bushmills*, is a powerful aid in retaining good health and warding off the attacks of seasonal ailments" — to advice on making punch — "Place a teaspoon in each tumbler to prevent cracking; pour in hot water to heat tumblers, then empty out; half fill tumblers with boiling water; add two lumps of sugar and a slice of lemon in each; fill up with *Old Bushmills*.".

These were the years when the Company further extended its markets not only to the United States and Canada but also to the Middle East and India. In a Cairo newspaper of January 1928, a Mr. Victor H. Frank of "Societe Omnia" announced that he had just been appointed sole agent in Egypt for *Old Bushmills*. On May 12, 1928 The Times of India carried "A Notice to Irishmen. . . It is now possible for you to obtain supplies of the best old Irish whiskey, shipped by the *Old Bushmills* Distillery, which has been famous since 1784." A case of three-star cost 75 Rupees, while 15 year-old "Black Bush" cost 86 Rupees. There were advertisements also in newspapers ranging from Montreal to Capetown, and from the Overseas Daily Mail to the now defunct Northern Whig in Belfast.

There was also a fascinating piece of advice from Mark Twain, who incidentally would have known about *Old Bushmills* during his visit to the Giant's Causeway — "I've had lots of trouble in my life, but most of it never happened!"

"OLD BUSHMILLS"

CELEBRATED

OLD IRISH WHISKY.

We have pleasure in announcing our appointment as Sole Agents for this superior quality Irish Whisky which has been famous since 1784.

We are confident that this Whisky will find a ready sale wherever there is a demand for a good Irish Whisky.

Sole Agents: HERBERT, SON & Co., Ltd., BOMBAY & CALCUTTA.

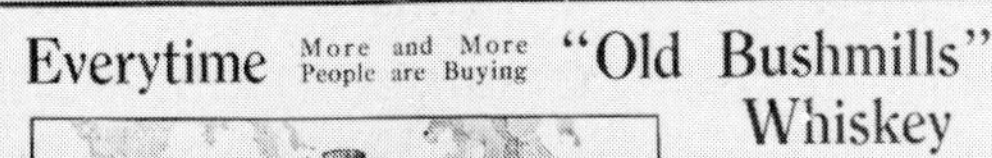

They know they can depend on its purity, maturity and sterling first class quality.

"Old Bushmills" Whiskey is good—not once, but always—that is why more people buy it, like it, and recommend it to their friends. It is so good everytime you try it.

Buy The Home Product
Buy "Bushmills"

THE "OLD BUSHMILLS" DISTILLERY CO., Ltd., Head Office: 5 23 HILL STREET, BELFAST

GLASGOW OFFICE—50 WELLINGTON STREET. LONDON OFFICE—74 GT. TOWER STREET.

WEAR ULSTER SHIRTS AND COLLARS.

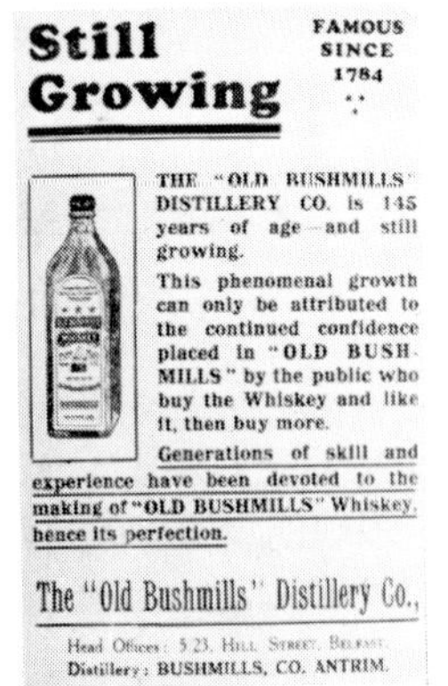

The Company extended its markets and its advertising not only to the United States, Canada and Britain, but also to the Middle East and India. And many advertisements were carried in local publications which had references to former landmarks like the Belfast Empire Theatre which, sadly, have long since disappeared.

And there was also some clerical humour in a local newspaper published in July, 1928. "Speaking at an installation service in Bushmills, the Reverend S. McCully, B.A., said his heart almost leaped within him as he traversed familiar roads and thought he was moving forward steadily towards old Bushmills (loud laughter). 'I am surprised' he added, amid further laughter, 'that the congregation, after nine years experience of me, should take that meaning out of my words!' "

The momentum and drive of the Company was maintained after Samuel Wilson Boyd's death by his sons Wilson, who became managing director and chairman, and his youngest son Austen, a director and later his older brother's successor. Robert, the eldest boy, had been injured playing rugby and never recovered fully from a kick in the kidneys. On occasions he went to stay with his sister Lillian in Philadelphia during the winter but was never well enough to go into the family business. He eventually married and settled at Whitehead. Another brother, Cecil, joined the Royal Ulster Rifles (36th Division) after he left Campbell College school. He was Commissioned as a Second-Lieutenant and went to France, where he was killed when he was only 18.

The other brother Clifford also joined the Army during the First World War as an officer in the North Irish Horse. He also went to France where he transferred to the Royal Flying Corps. He survived the war, but his health was permanently impaired by his experiences. He joined the *Old Bushmills* Company in the early Twenties and became a director. There is little doubt that had his health been better and had he remained with the firm he would have succeeded Wilson as managing director. But he left the Company around 1947 and retired to a farm which he had bought near Hillsborough.

Shrewd

Wilson Boyd quickly made his mark as a shrewd businessman and a character larger than life. Soon after he took over the business he went to America to help revitalise the market for Irish whiskey following the end of Prohibition. Like his father he was an active anti-prohibitionist in Belfast. In May 1933 he wrote in "The Ulster Magazine"; "As far as a big majority of the States are concerned, the end of Prohibition is in sight. Our plans are of course well advanced, and I intend to sail shortly to conclude and get under way a complete distributing organisation."

Earlier the same year he was quoted by the Belfast Telegraph (March 1) during an Ulster Anti-Prohibition Rally. He criticised a local cleric who had claimed that the liquor trade, unlike other sectors of business and commerce during the First World War, had escaped Government rationing. Wilson Boyd pointed out forcefully that the output of beer was almost 3,000,000 barrels less in 1917 than the previous year, and that the 1917 output of spirits was 50 pc less than the 1916 clearances from bond. The report continued; "That was his answer to the fulminations of the Reverend T. M. Johnstone, and while he thought most people appraised that gentleman at his true worth, still it was well to keep the true facts before the public. (Applause)".

Boyd, no doubt like the reverend gentleman, was well able to fight his corner but those who knew him said that Wilson could be a most charming man, yet also a difficult person if crossed. He was flamboyant and generous, but in some ways parsimonious. His motto was "Look after the pennies and the pounds will look after themselves." He was generous to charity, yet he would quibble over paying certain professional fees partly because he disliked spending money that was not "productive." And yet his flamboyant style and generosity were well illustrated by a story from North Antrim. After visiting the Distillery at Coleraine, which he bought in 1933, he used to drop in at a local pub called "Mary Craigs." One day he found the barmaid in floods of tears. When he asked what she was crying about, she replied that she had got the sack. He stepped into the manager's office, where he spent some time. On coming out, he said to the girl "Dry your tears, you're not getting the sack after all". She asked him how he had managed this, and he replied "I've bought the place." And so he had! (Three years later Wilson Boyd also bought the Killowen Distillery in Coleraine).

Wilson and his wife Jessie, described by someone who knew her as 'lively with dancing dark eyes' and with extremely quick repartee, lived in a grand house at Marino, a fashionable suburb east of Belfast. They loved to entertain and an early fad was roller-skating with their friends in the drawing-room. The Boyds were childless, and this caused great sadness. Mrs. Janet Boyd says of her brother and sister-in-law. "If they had had children, things might have been different. Wilson was very fond of children, but he seemed embarrassed to show it." Nothing was ever said, but he was bound to have been keenly aware that his brother Austen and sister-in-law Janet had three sons.

The wedding picture of Wilson Boyd and his wife Jessie. Wilson, the second eldest son, succeeded his father in 1932 and was chairman and managing director for some thirty years. He was flamboyant and strong-willed. His wife was described by a contemporary as "lively with dancing dark eyes and with extremely quick repartee." The Wilson Boyds loved to entertain and an early fad was roller-skating with their friends in the drawing-room!

Garden

Wilson and his wife had a large garden and conservatory, both of which were kept in excellent condition by full-time staff. In every way possible, Wilson liked to make a show. He dressed well, and strikingly in a Homburg hat. He had a penchant for cars and at one stage owned four, including a Rolls-Royce. (Incidentally before the Boyd family had a car, they had a brougham driven by "Old Tom" the coachman, who was later employed as store-keeper at the offices. Apparently he did not take kindly to the idea of learning to drive a car instead of a horse!)

Wilson Boyd with a bottle of a favourite product. He was a big man, with style. He was a good businessman and a first-class salesman. He was also a strict employer, and on occasions a difficult man to cross. But overall his contribution to the story of "Old Bushmills" during the years of world upheaval and business challenge was immense. He was known to the Belfast employees as "The Guv'nor."

Wilson Boyd's flamboyant style, and his ability to laugh at himself, were exemplified in the story about an important American visitor who stayed at his home at Marino. He had just fitted out a splendid second bathroom when he discovered that the local supply from a well had run dry. So Wilson Boyd instructed a lorry driver from Bushmills to load up casks filled with water and to replenish the tank. The guest duly arrived, and decided to have a bath before his evening meal. He came down for dinner somewhat puzzled. "That was a terrific bath" he said "but you sure have special water in this part of the world. I could swear that I had a whiff of whiskey as I washed myself." And he certainly had! All Wilson Boyd could do was to own up, and to share the joke against himself.

Though affable to friends and guests, Wilson Boyd was a strict employer. He was described by one man as "a benevolent despot!" The Hill Street headquarters were more than a little Dickensian. There were only two private offices — one originally for old Samuel Wilson Boyd and the other for the eldest son, though in fact occupied by Wilson. The other sons had their desks in the large general offices. Clerks on high stools sat filling in ledgers mostly around the edges of the room where the light was best. Typists and sons were in the middle, and the sons' desks were nearest the fire at the far end.

Kenneth Boyd, the youngest of the three sons of Austen and Janet Boyd, later worked at the Distillery. He recalls the atmosphere of the Hill Street headquarters of the firm. "My first impression was that of an old-fashioned place. There were huge ledgers being filled in by hand, and a great deal of dust. People did not exactly wear wing-collars but there were quite a number who had worked there for a very long time and who had known my grandfather. The chief clerk was a Mr. Tully, and he was a great character. He was a tall, rather severe-looking person, but a terribly kind man, and awfully good to me."

"People in the Hill Street office worked very hard. During the week it was obligatory to wear a suit. A sports jacket and flannels were allowed at the weekends. Smoking, however, was not allowed — in theory. In practice I used to nip round to the warehouse to enjoy a quiet smoke with the duty-free officer!"

Hard work

Other people who worked in the Hill Street office confirm this atmosphere of hard work and discipline, though pleasantly so. Bertie Gifford started working in Hill Street as an apprentice in 1931. He later became a salesman and stayed with the Company all his working life, some 40 years.

"When I came in as an office apprentice at 15 I was at everybody's beck and call. I had to have the books on peoples' desks without delay in the mornings — and I worked from nine in the morning to six in the evening, and sometimes an awful lot longer. I had to wait until all the letters were signed and take them down to the Waring Street Post Office. And this was all for the princely sum of £20 a year!"

Alex McNally started in 1927, also as an apprentice, and stayed with the Company for 44 years. "You had to know your job or you would not have been kept on. They were very particular on all aspects of the business. It was not the sort of place where

A wedding photograph of Austen, youngest of the five surviving sons of Samuel Wilson Boyd. Austen later became chairman and managing director of "Old Bushmills." He and his wife Janet met on a world cruise, and were married in London on January 3, 1930. Mrs Janet Boyd, an American from Albany in New York State, recalls; "As soon as I arrived in 1930 I bought a bicycle on which I rode all over Belfast and the adjacent country. This was a great way of getting to know the place; and when one knows, one loves."

BOYD&Co
BELFAST
BOYD&Co
BELFAST
BOYD&Co
BELFAST

War, though catastrophic in human and social terms, led to even greater demand for *Old Bushmills* which unfortunately became scarce due to Government rationing of barley.

As well, the Company lost entire floors of matured whiskey when the Hill Street premises and the bonded warehouse at Gordon Street were hit during a Luftwaffe raid on Belfast in 1941. Alex McNally and Bertie Gifford remember well the dark days of war. Gifford recalls; "Three weeks previously the Government advised us to get rid of our stock because something like that was likely to happen. But it was a major job to clear entire floors of whiskey in so short a time. During the air attack the bond stores suffered a direct hit, and up went the whiskey. It was as precious as gold dust. The fire smouldered for about a week and the heat was so intense that some of the steel beams were twisted like pins."

Limited

McNally remembers that supplies became even more limited after 1942. "The Government refused to allow us grain for distilling because it was badly needed for food, so we had to conserve our stocks even further. We started by trying to supply our regular customers with 100 pc of their 1940 quota, but within two years this had dropped to 17½ per cent of the 1940 figures. Wilson Boyd then said 'We'll make "Black Bush" so expensive that people won't be able to buy it' but that only increased the demand! We could have sold all we had and more, but we had to conserve stocks for the future. There was no trouble about customers paying cash. They had to pay in advance, and they were extremely glad to get it."

There was also a great deal of financial speculation, and whiskey fetched huge prices on the black market. McNally recalls whiskey increasing from 10 shillings a proof gallon to more than 200 shillings, by the end of the war. The *Old Bushmills* export quota was sold to American forces who were stationed in Northern Ireland, most of them prior to the Allied landings in Europe.

The Second World War changed the political map of Europe and the ravages of the conflict left scars that have yet to heal. Another generation fought and was killed or injured in far-flung theatres of war. The world itself became a little older but, arguably, hardly more wise. Yet paradoxically the War, as from 1914 to 1918, actually helped the whiskey business. The Boyds were faced with much the same problem as their predecessors — stocks of whiskey that had been laid down long before the outbreak of war had increased dramatically in value and the Company faced the prospect of yet another windfall tax by the Government. It was a time when the Boyds were willing to consider a reasonable offer, and such an offer came, though in odd circumstances.

Isaac Wolfson, the self-made textile magnate, owned several business concerns in the North of Ireland. During the war a Belfast stockbroker Mr. Joseph Boyd, was able to supply him with whiskey for his guests. (Wolfson's taste rarely went beyond a glass of sherry.) Shortly after the war he attended a business lunch in Belfast's Grand Central Hotel where he met Wilson Boyd. When he heard the name, Wolfson assumed that this was the Mr. Boyd who had been supplying him with whiskey. So

Director

Austen Boyd was also a director of the Falls Flax Spinning Company Ltd. and Irish Linen Mills Limited, a reflection on his younger days when he seemed destined to make a career in the textile trade. His widow Mrs. Janet Boyd says "He had broken his foot in a hunting accident and he was not able to work for at least a year. He wanted to go back into textiles but his father needed him in distilling, and that was that."

During the Second World War he joined the Harbour Patrol and was in command of two vessels which were sent out at night as trouble-shooters. In 1941 he became Assistant Command Welfare Officer for Northern Ireland. His widow recalls; "He served first as Captain, and then as Major but without pay!' However, he was free to leave at any time. It was a hectic life, dashing across Belfast from his Bushmills office in Hill Street to the welfare office in Bedford Street, and on certain days — when he was on the road — not getting to any office. He acted as a liaison officer between Army and civilians, he looked after canteens, entertainment for the troops, and family welfare. He also acted as liaison officer between the British and American troops in Northern Ireland and around 1942 he even staged American baseball and football to raise money for charity."

Austen Boyd's qualities as a quiet reconciler were illustrated by his work as chairman of the Joint Committee of the Red Cross and St. John Ambulance and he was awarded the Red Cross Society's highest honour — life membership. He was also extremely interested in the world of medicine and was a distinguished Chairman of the Belfast Hospitals Management Committee. The then new Outpatients Department at the Royal Victoria Hospital was named after him, and the family retains as a treasured heirloom the goblet specially inscribed with a picture of Bushmills which was presented to him on that occasion. His son Kenneth says "I believe that this was one of the proudest days of his life."

(My own recollection of Austen Boyd, whom I met shortly before his death in 1973, was that of a man of great old-world charm. I was carrying out research for a book about the work of Northern Ireland hospitals during the sustained outbreak of violence since 1969 and I joined Mr. Boyd for lunch in the consultants' dining-room at the Royal Victoria Hospital. He said, in measured tones approaching a kind of reverence, "You do realise, young man, that you are now sitting at the heart of Ulster medicine!" Austen Boyd was typical of a generation of men who had made their mark in business and commerce and who gave remarkable and voluntary service to many of the great institutions of their country.)

Affection

During his later years Mrs. Boyd joined him on business trips to Europe and North America. She remembers him, not unnaturally, with great affection. "He had considerable business ability and I believe he inherited his father's business acumen. Austen was a kind, modest and essentially a humble person. He was not a pretender. He never tried to pretend to be anything or to have anything that he was not or did

Mrs. Janet Boyd holding a goblet presented to her late husband Austen. "He was a kind, modest and essentially a humble person." The goblet, which is engraved with a picture of Bushmills, was presented to Austen Boyd to mark the opening of the new Outpatients Department at the Royal Victoria Hospital in Belfast. Mr. Boyd was a former Chairman of the Belfast Hospitals Management Committee. His son Kenneth remembers the presentation; "I believe that this was one of the proudest days of his life."

"Old Bushmills" which survived for centuries under one or other small local Ulster proprietor moved within a relatively few years from one large business empire to another. It retained its distinctive old-world character but also applied the latest techniques of management.

CHAPTER SIX

"Big Business"

Lord Macaulay, the 19th century Whig historian, once summarised neatly the golden rule that helps to sell newspapers — "A broken head in Cold Bath Fields produces a greater sensation among us than three pitched battles in India." On the morning of Friday July 17, 1964 the same axiom was applied to the "News Letter." The front-page banner headline announced major local news; *"Old Bushmills* sold in £1½ m takeover. Ulster whiskey will have 5,000 new outlets."

The story ran thus; "*Old Bushmills,* the only whiskey distilling company left in Northern Ireland, has been bought for £1,550,000 by the Charrington United Breweries Group, who are to 'plug' its products in their 5,000 bars and off-licences in Britain. Charringtons, who already own the Ulster brewery, bought *Old Bushmills* from Sir Isaac Wolfson's Drages Company for £750,000 cash and a million shares in Charrington United.

"A spokesman for *Old Bushmills* said yesterday 'This could lead to more employment and also to the use of more Ulster barley which will, naturally, benefit the farmer. We visualise a vast expansion.' 'Bush', which is produced by 100 workers in several small distilleries in Northern Ireland is the best-selling Irish brand in the United States, Canada and the British West Indies, and it has already begun to capture palates in West Germany, Italy and Austria. Charrington's are one of the largest groups of brewers in the United Kingdom and have given an assurance that the existing management will continue to operate the business."

The newspaper's London editor noted that Charrington's had begun brewing "in a small way" in 1757, that in 1964 its employees (apart from public house licensees and their workers) exceeded 10,000 people, that the company had 4,900 licensed premises and 655 off-licenses, and "that after more than a couple of hundred years, there is still a Charrington as the head of the company — John Charrington."

Thus ended the newspaper report which stimulated conversation over breakfast and later in boardrooms throughout Ulster, where the news about the past, present and likely future of one of its best-known institutions was greeted with surprise and speculation. There was surprise among those who had not known that *Old Bushmills* had been part of the Wolfson empire, and there was speculation from those who asked how a brewing company would develop a Distillery, and why Charringtons had been interested in *Old Bushmills* in the first place. That surprise and speculation was evident also among many *Old Bushmills* employees themselves who first read the news from their morning paper.

CITY FINAL

NEWS LETTER

Telephone Belfast 33633 | Friday, July 17, 1964 | Price 3d

Ulster whiskey will have 5,000 new outlets

OLD BUSHMILLS SOLD IN £1½m. TAKE-OVER

By a News Letter reporter

Old Bushmills, the only whiskey distilling company left in Northern Ireland, has been bought for £1,550,000 by Charrington United Breweries Group, who are to "plug" its products in their 5,000 bars and off-licences in Britain.

Charrington's, who already own the Ulster Brewery, bought Old Bushmills from Sir Isaac Wolfson's Drages Company for £750,000 cash and million shares in Charrington United.

A spokesman for Old Bushmills said yesterday: "This will lead to more employment and also the use of more Ulster barley, which will, naturally, benefit the farmer. We visualise a vast expansion."

"Bush," which is produced by 100 workers in several distilleries in Northern Ireland, is the best-selling brand in the United States, Canada and the British West Indies, and it has already begun to capture palates in West Germany, Italy and Austria.

... history that the origins have been lost in the annals of time.

The first mention of intoxicating liquor in Ireland, in an ancient work called the Book of Leinster, concerns a feast at Dundabheann, near Bushmills, where some of the guests imbibed the local distillation so freely that, on leaving at midnight, they started out for Louth on the east coast and never knew where they were until they reached County Limerick.

Whiskey is eminently an Irish product. The word comes from the old Irish "Uisge Bheatha," water of life.

Campbell's Bluebird lifts speed record to 403 m.p.h.

At Lake Eyre in South Australia this morning, Donald Campbell broke the 17-year-old world land speed record in his car Bluebird.

Bluebird was timed twice through the measured mile on the Lake Eyre salt track at 403.1 m.p.h. The previous world record was 394.196 m.p.h. set by the late John Cobb in Utah in 1947.

Bluebird was timed officially at 403.1 m.p.h. through the measured mile and 388.7 m.p.h. through the measured kilometre in its first run shortly after sunrise. On the return run, Bluebird sped through the mile at 403.1 m.p.h.—identical to the first mile speed—and through the kilometre at 400.5 m.p.h.

Wife witness

An elated Campbell jumped from Bluebird after the second run and embraced his wife Tonia, who had watched the record bid from the track side.

"Darling, we've done it," Campbell cried.

He said he was disappointed that he had not broken the American unofficial record speed of 407 m.p.h. set in a jet-propelled three-wheeled vehicle last August.

Bluebird officials moving down the track after the record run found pieces of rubber, about matchbox size. They were believed to have come from Bluebird's rear right tyre.

RUGBY STAR FOR CYPRUS

When Mr. Austin Hewitt, 26-year-old Ulster rugby winger, applied for a job as one of Belfast's three new Y.M.C.A. youth leaders he little thought that his first two months training would be spent in the strife-torn island of Cyprus.

Brother of David Hewitt, the Irish international, Austin has played for Instonians and Queen's University.

Since leaving the university he has been working in an estate agent's office in Belfast, but he told me last night: "I decided that this was not my niche. I know working with people and property dealing was a bit limiting. Part-time youth work has been my big interest and when the Y.M.C.A. advertised these posts I decided to apply.

Staffing

"A short time ago I received a telephone call from the Y.M.C.A. who said there was an emergency in Cyprus. I said I had heard about it," said Mr. Hewitt laughingly, "but they said it was not that emergency, but one of staffing in their Cyprus branch at the British base at Episkopi."

"What will I be doing? Mainly providing mobile canteens and recreation for the Servicemen and

First with a difference

Trevor Fox, Birmingham businessman, runner-up in the 1962 European championships, and Jeremy James, ... for the 18½ mile crossing from Portpatrick to Donaghadee yesterday.

No records likely in our

£220 talent competition winners

The Seekers, a beat group from Newcastle, Co. Down, won the first heat in the group section of the Gallaher-sponsored £220 talent competition at the Arcadia Ballroom, Port-

News Letter Mini—35 in grand final.

SEE PAGE 7

However, such developments would not have been totally surprising to those who had kept open a weather-eye for visitors in the sleepy seaside quaintness of North Antrim. They might have noticed, for example, two distinguished-looking gentlemen driving around the Bushmills area in a Mercedes car, and having lunch at the Bayview Hotel in Portballintrae. One was Sir Robin Kinahan, a member of a family long-established in the wines and spirits trade and a former Lord Mayor of Belfast. The other was the same John Charrington mentioned in the newspaper story. Both were making a quiet reconnaisance of *Old Bushmills* prior to the take-over.

Take-over

John Charrington, however, was not a stranger to the North in general. He had been stationed near Antrim with a Yeomanry Regiment during the Second World War, and his second wife was from Newry. Sir Robin Kinahan, who was a Director of Charrington United Breweries and later Chairman of *Old Bushmills* recalled; "John was fond of this part of the world. He liked the North Coast physically and he was extremely keen on the Distillery. Charringtons already had two distilleries in Scotland, they were anxious to develop elsewhere and *Old Bushmills* seemed right for them."

Both men related well on a personal level, and Sir Robin later paid tribute to Charrington's qualities — "A magnificent person, a most gentlemanly Christian and a fine businessman." He was also rather patriotic and suggested that Kinahan might consider changing his German Mercedes for a British car. From that time on Sir Robin drove a Rover!

Though the initial announcement of the Charrington take-over was greeted with surprise by many people, it was obvious to any knowledgeable observer of the distilling industry that long-term security lay with the comparative security of the larger business empires. The days of the small, family businesses and one-man concerns were over. A census in 1813 showed that there were about 20,000 illicit stills in Ireland. When Alfred Barnard came to Ireland in the late nineteenth century he visited 28 distilleries, though only one of these proprietors — a William Higgin of Avoniel in Belfast showed him out of the door. "The proprietor stands conspicuous as being unwilling to allow an inspection of his works — for what reason we are unable to explain," wrote Barnard rather sadly.[1]

Undaunted

Undaunted, however, he proceeded in his 1887 publication to describe no less than six distilleries in Dublin; one each at Monasterevin, Tullamore, Kilbeggan, Galway, Limerick; two in Cork; one at Bandon and Midleton, one at Parsonstown, Wexford and Dundalk; two in Belfast (and Avoniel by default!); two in Comber, two in Londonderry, one at Limavady, and, as mentioned elsewhere, the distilleries at Bushmills and Coleraine. Yet only 77 years later, all the Northern distilleries with the exception of *Old Bushmills* and Coleraine had disappeared. The motto was clear — consolidate or perish! As E. B. McGuire notes in his standard work on Irish whiskey; "In the modern world the days of the small individually-owned distillery are over. The capital needed to survive is far too much."[2] He further notes; "In 1926 . . . there were twelve distilleries in Northern Ireland producing nearly two million gallons . . . By 1950 only the smaller potstill distilleries in Bushmills, Coleraine and Comber remained, and Comber ceased distilling in 1953."[3]

The demise of the smaller distilleries and the reasons for such developments include the considerable rise in spirit duties during this century, the adverse effect of the Immature Spirits (Restriction) Act of 1915, the strong competition from Scotch blends, the "boom and bust" cycles of the whiskey business and, not least, the competition among Irish distillers themselves. A detailed survey of such factors is beyond the scope of this book but the history is well documented by McGuire in his volume.[4]

So when Charringtons took over *Old Bushmills* in 1964 it was a guarantee, if nothing else, about continuity in an industry that had all but disappeared in the North and, to a lesser extent in the Republic compared to the more heady days of previous centuries. It was significant, too, that in the brewing business amalgamation was also the order of the day. The Ulster Brewery Company, a consortium of Ulster vintners, was taken over by Northern Breweries Ltd. With the acquisition of several other breweries it became United Breweries, and eventually merged with Charrington to form Charrington United Breweries. Then with the acquisition of the local firm of Lyle and Kinahan, the wines and spirit merchants who had been in business for 112 years, and *Old Bushmills* the name changed to Charrington Kinahan Ltd. Later it became Bass Charrington (Ireland) Ltd. The present name, Bass Ireland Ltd, dates from 1974 and although the official connection with *Old Bushmills* has disappeared, the personal relationships between both companies and staff remain close.

Human face

Details of mergers may seem impersonal and indeed clinical business transactions at boardroom level, but it is left to human beings to implement such decisions in the everyday affairs of a company and its employees. Thus when the details of the Charrington acquisition had graced, however briefly, the newspapers and when readers' attention was focused elsewhere, it was left to Peter Chester-Williams and others to help implement the new policy at *Old Bushmills*.

The son of a consultant radiologist from Yorkshire, Chester-Williams trained in the brewery business in England before transferring to Belfast. He was appointed personal assistant to Sir Robin Kinahan, and became production manager at *Old Bushmills*. "My job was to co-ordinate the work of the two Distilleries and also to co-ordinate the capital investment programme we planned to carry out. But in no way was I trying to tell people how to make whiskey!".

"The Distilleries had been run and managed under the old traditions. In many respects the buildings and plant were antiquated and the impression was of a production that was not geared to massive expansion. Initially, I felt that I was very much the outsider but the people were kindly disposed towards me. There was always the feeling of a pride in the job, of a well-ordered place where people came to do a day's work and made the best of what they had. I learned a great deal from my experience at *Old Bushmills*. I was just over 30 and it was my first taste of being the man on the spot. My lasting impression was of people who knew that they made a good product. It was in their bones. The quality was always there."

Expansion

One of the major decisions was to close the bottling-hall in the Coleraine Distillery and to develop a new blending and bottling area at Bushmills. This was part of a £1.25 million expansion. On May 23, 1966 the new bonded warehouse was opened officially by His Excellency the Lord Erskine of Rerrick, the Governor of Northern Ireland, and the Company announced that the second phase of expansion would be completed in the Spring of 1967. On schedule, the new bottling and blending department was opened, appropriately by the Rt Hon, the Lord Coleraine on Monday, 6 November 1967. The official programme on that day outlined what had been achieved since 1965.

The "Old Bushmills" Distillery Company Limited

The Opening of

A NEW BOTTLING AND BLENDING DEPARTMENT

by

The Rt. Hon. The Lord Coleraine, LL.D.

Monday 6th November 1967

"With the completion of the new Number 3 Warehouse in the autumn of 1965, preparations were made to start on the second phase of the Bushmills Distillery expansion programme. The construction of a new Bottling and Blending Department together with a new Warehouse commenced in the summer of 1966, and the work was completed by the builders — Hugh Taggart and Sons, Ballymoney — in July 1967.

"The new buildings cover a total area of 32,000 sq ft and this is divided between the Bottling Department, 14,348 sq ft, Blend area 5,439 sq ft and New Warehouse 12,213 sq ft. The Blend Area has been connected to Number 3 Warehouse to enable easy access for storage of blends, and the removal of bottlings. Tipping troughs are used for emptying casks. The new stainless steel blend tank (capacity 7,500 gallons) gives adequate capacity for any variations in our future requirements."

"The Bottling Department is divided into the materials store, its associated loading bay, the Bottling Hall and its loading bay. The materials store is used solely for the storage of bottling materials, the walls being racked to hold pallets four high. The central area is left free for block storage of bottles. Bottles and cartons are fed on separate conveyors from the materials store directly into the Bottling Hall. The Bottling Hall has, at present, a single line in operation with a capacity of up to 350 dozen per hour. There is, however, adequate space available for a second line when required. The four bottling tanks give adequate flexibility for the different bottlings of *Old Bushmills.*

"In addition to the Bottling and Blending Department a new Warehouse has been built with a total capacity of 500,000 proof gallons. As in Number 3 Warehouse, casks are stowed ten high on individual rails. At the present moment only half the Warehouse has been racked to meet our immediate requirements."

Prose

This deathless prose may be of detailed interest to the social and industrial historian, but those who attended the opening had the benefit of local refreshments to ease them through such statistics of development! However, the Company's announcements on sales at that period made rather more stimulating reading. "Considerable success was attained with sales during 1965; exports to America were increased by 25%, and sales to the home market . . . by 19%. Sales have continued to increase in all markets during 1966. Particular success has been achieved again in the American market where exports have shown a 49% increase over the same period last year. It is anticipated that total sales during 1966 will increase by 36%.

That sharp edge to the sales drive was personified by Kevin Murphy who was part of the 'hungry-fighter' syndrome and who began at the bottom end of the licensed business before eventually becoming Chairman of Bass Ireland Ltd. During his days as a traveller on the road he had gained a healthy respect for *Old Bushmills* as a product, and for Wilson Boyd as an operator. Murphy remembers; "Wilson Boyd kept a diary on all his customers. He made about a dozen calls a day and before he went in he consulted his 'oracle'. He knew all about the man's young son, or ailing wife, or a daughter who was bright at school. He built up such friendly relationships that it was just as if he had resumed a conversation that had been broken off earlier. He impressed me tremendously — here was a man who knew what 'personality selling' was all about, long before the term had been invented."

"My experience of those days taught me great lessons. I learned from the successful salesmen that everyone in the business was important. They would take time to talk to the youngest apprentice. I was told 'He may be the apprentice today, but some day he may own the place or another establishment. So treat him accordingly'."

With a determined drive, Murphy and his team improved the sales of *Old Bushmills.* He recalls; "I put Charles Taylor in charge of sales down South and he did a fantastic job. It was a Northern product, we were proud of it and we really wanted to 'turn it on!' When we took over we were selling 24,000 cases each year in the North alone, including 10% of "Black Bush". When we handed over the business some seven years later we were selling about 124,000 cases in the North. So we really had done our 'party piece'."

Paradox

Despite the comparative success in sales, the inbuilt paradox of a brewing company developing a Distillery had not been resolved. Brewers by training are accustomed to a relatively quick return on investment, whereas distillers are prepared to wait for years while their stocks slowly mature in the warehouse. Many of the company employees felt that while Charringtons had expanded *Old Bushmills* their long-term interests lay best with a group whose primary concern was distilling.

In the early Seventies two developments made news, perhaps not in the best possible way but they were all part of the story of *Old Bushmills.* On one occasion a series of errors led to a quantity of spirits being discharged into the River Bush, with unknown repercussions for North Antrim salmon. It resulted, among other things, in a phone call from John Charrington, who had just read his Sunday newspaper, to Sir Robin Kinahan asking politely what they were doing to his *Old Bushmills* and to the fish! Steps were taken to prevent such an occurrence ever happening again.

A rather more serious development was a shortage of "Black Bush" liqueur whiskey due to a rapid depletion of existing stocks, but happily the considerable increase in production later on made up for this leeway. But there was consternation among those of good taste, for whom "Black Bush" became, temporarily, like gold dust.

In an overall context, Kevin Murphy notes; "Charringtons had many interests and so many priorities. They decided to get out of the production of Scotch whisky and they acquired an agency for Vat 69. In no time at all they were selling 150,000 cases a year without having to make investments in stock, and with no worries about whether they were over-stocking or not. It seemed to me that the writing was on the wall and that it was only a matter of time before they sold the *Old Bushmills* Distillery." He was soon proved right!

Largest

The Seagram Company Ltd, which is based in Montreal, is the world's largest producer and distributor of distilled spirits and wines, and it acquired *Old Bushmills* from Charringtons in a high-level deal. There was regret among the local Bass-Charrington management that *Old Bushmills* was sold in this way. (Ironically, even today, outside visitors to Bass Ireland are sent home with a special present which reminds them particularly of Ulster — a bottle of "Black Bush"!) Even if the local Bass-Charrington management had been consulted in depth about the proposed take-over in 1972, there seems to have been little they could have done. Kevin

Murphy sums up philosophically; "Charringtons did best out of beer and that's where their major investments went. It became known through the grapevine that they were going to sell the *Old Bushmills* Distillery, and local management were voices in the wilderness. When I heard that it had been bought by Seagram, it seemed to be good sense for a company which may have been intending to do for *Old Bushmills* what Chivas Regal has done for Scotch."

However, *Old Bushmills* was not destined to become an Irish 'Chivas Regal'. In another complicated deal the Distillery gradually moved under the control of the Irish Distillers Group. Thus a local company which had survived for centuries under one or other small Ulster proprietor had moved within a relatively few years from one large business empire to another. Although it might not have been obvious at the time, each development pushed *Old Bushmills* more firmly into the world of big business with its large investments and sophisticated marketing and management. In so doing it gradually acquired the best of both worlds — it retained its distinctive old-world character but behind the scenes it applied the latest techniques of management and the disciplines of corporate survival, within the Irish Distillers Group.

Amalgamation

The Irish Distillers Group was formed in 1966 but a century earlier the commercial advantages of amalgamation were underlined when four distilleries in Cork city and the Midleton distillery nearby joined together to become the Cork Distilleries Company. The famous names of Power, Jameson, Cork and Tullamore merged in the mid-Sixties, and *Old Bushmills* was to join them in the early Seventies but long before such a formal structure had been established there had been a 'de facto' relationship across the Irish border, albeit among competitors.

Stephen Murphy, a director of the Irish Distillers Group and a member of a family with a long proprietorial history in Cork, recalls meeting Wilson Boyd of *Old Bushmills* during his visits North and at the regular meetings of The Irish Pot Still Distillers Association, with members from North and South. Stephen Murphy, who talks entertainingly about the whiskey business, forged his own personal links with the North, both by spending a walking holiday in the Mournes at the height of the disturbances and much earlier by indulging his passion for rugby football. In March, 1948, he was fortunate enough to secure a ticket for the historic international in Belfast when Ireland beat Wales 6-3 to win the Triple Crown, for the first time since 1899!

Another man who recalls a visit to *Old Bushmills* is Sandy Ross, the site superintendent at Midleton. He is the son of a former distiller at the old Midleton distillery and he remembers well the atmosphere and the character of the old establishment. (One of Sandy's forbears is mentioned by Alfred Barnard in his description of the Midleton Distillery). As a man who was reared in the whiskey business he has all the essentials of blending and distilling at his finger-tips, and he will show the visitor with pride the biggest potstill in the world — the now disused 31,648 gallon still at Midleton. Sandy also has a remarkable tale of personal survival. When the old Midleton distillery was in operation a potstill blew up, and he was hurled down the stillroom and out through a window by the blast. He was left wearing only the collar of his shirt and the belt of his coat! Legend relates that one of the family bosses commiserated with him and advised him to take the rest of the day off — but to be sure to report for work the next morning!

In 1968 Sandy spent a summer holiday in the North, and he visited the *Old Bushmills* Distillery incognito. He says "In those days we were competitors, so I did not feel like driving up and announcing who I was. I joined this tour party but it may have been evident from my questions that I knew more about the business than the ordinary tourist! The result was that I ended up in the office of Austen Boyd, who was most charming. I remember him opening a safe and producing a bottle of *Old Bushmills*. He gave my companion and me the rest of the bottle to take with us, and also a model of a Bushmills potstill." That model potstill rests today in Sandy Ross's local — "The Stables", a hostelry near Midleton, which also keeps a supply of *Old Bushmills* for regular customers. Thus, although the formal grouping of Irish distillers was consolidated in the Sixties and Seventies, there were the personal contacts and the human stories of mutual interest which has helped to give the distilling business its special character.

Sandy Ross, site superintendent with Irish Distillers in Cork, comes from a family with a long history in distilling. When he visited "Old Bushmills" in the late Sixties he was given a model of a potstill. Today it rests in his favourite hostelry near Midleton, Cork.

Key figure

One man who helped to carve out a distinct identity for the new company was Kevin McCourt, who retired as group managing director in 1978, having been brought in ten years earlier as an independent, non-whiskey family, managing director. He had the task of welding together the three family firms which had merged in 1966. To do this, he not only had to rationalise the organisation, but also to create a sense of teamwork at all levels among employees who for generations had been competing fiercely with one another.

He brought to the group a very wide business background. This included a period as Director-General of Radio Telefis Eireann, the national broadcasting organisation, and valuable international experience with Hunter Douglas, an engineering firm based in Holland.

It was McCourt's contact with Seagram executives that eventually secured *Old Bushmills* for Irish Distillers, and completed the amalgamation of the Irish whiskey industry, which took shape from 1966 onwards.

During his ten years at the helm of the group, the Irish distilling industry was completely revitalised. Whilst he had the complete support of a progressive Board, nonetheless his powers of persuasion and the force of his personality clinched many an argument along the way. To a great number of his associates, McCourt was larger-than-life, and a dynamic man with an unswerving belief in the potential and future of the Irish whiskey industry.

In personal terms he was a strict disciplinarian, and a stickler for protocol. This was balanced by his charm and his ability to make people believe in themselves.

After he relinquished his position as managing director he remained a director until his retirement in 1983. As a key figure in the formative years of the group, Kevin McCourt is also an important part of the long story of *Old Bushmills*.

Kevin McCourt (left) and Frank O'Reilly who each played an important role in their own ways with the Irish Distillers' Group.

Dynamic

Another man who played an important role in the group was Frank O'Reilly, who retired from the chairmanship in 1983 after seventeen years' service, and was succeeded by Dr. Michael Killeen, former managing director of the Irish Industrial Development Authority.

O'Reilly was one of those engaging and dynamic men who seem to thrive on challenges. Like so many others in distilling, he had strong family ties — his grandmother was one of the Powers — and his early training provided an invaluable experience for his key role in the boardroom later on.

He qualified as an engineer from Trinity College in Dublin and served during the Second World War with the Royal Engineers in the Seventh Indian Division in South East Asia — "it gave me a wonderful background in human relations" — but his heart lay in distilling. He recalled "It was in one's blood. The only thing I didn't do in those days was bottling, but I remember the old coal-fired stills, the characters, and the sense of craftsmanship, and I cannot think of another industry where so many different crafts were brought together. When you worked with these men you could not help but respect their expertise and dedication, whether malting, milling or distilling. It always has been an industry with its roots in the soil and many of the workers had been connected with the land for generations. There was a great father and son tradition and a sense of loyalty. Many of the things I have seen at *Old Bushmills,* I experienced years ago at Powers — the character, the dedication, the camaraderie and the atmosphere."

Frank O'Reilly moved from production to senior management. "I did not set out to go into management, but I suppose it was a natural step. I missed mixing with former colleagues and with some of the old characters. But I began to learn about finance and about marketing." He became chairman of Powers, at a time when the old family houses were competing with one another and making little impression on the world market.

Streamlined

They were working against one another and simply weren't big enough to make their presence felt sufficiently in the outside world. So the common interest of streamlining the business and making a greater co-ordinated effort helped to draw together the threads of an amalgamation, and this became a reality in 1966. Significantly, however, *Old Bushmills* remained outside. It had not been forgotten but an acquisition was not possible at that time. The company was not for sale. Ironically, the intervention of an outsider — Seagram of Canada — made it possible eventually to gather the production and marketing of all Irish whiskey under one umbrella.

Initially, Seagram had a 100 pc interest in *Old Bushmills* but in a series of moves which seem complicated to the layman but apparently are not so in practice, the Irish Distillers Group gradually bought over the whole company. In return Seagrams gained a 20 pc holding in Irish Distillers, and in an underlying shareholding agreement they undertook not to increase their stake — thus

The Irish Distillers Group comprises one of the world's newest distillery plants and (above) at "Old Bushmills" the world's oldest licensed whiskey distillery currently in production.

guaranteeing Irish Distillers' continued independence and freedom of action as a major Irish public company.

It was clear from the late Sixties that the existing Irish distilleries needed to be modernised and expanded to meet the increasing world demand. However, the expansion of the Jameson and Power distilleries in built-up areas of Dublin was well-nigh impossible. As well, the geographical distance between the Cork and Dublin distilleries led to administrative and management problems. So the group began to search for a new central production site, and eventually settled in an area of 110 acres at Midleton, near Cork. This is good cereal country, and Midleton has plentiful supplies of clear, pure water — the ingredients necessary for good distilling. Work began on the complex in April 1973 and finished in July 1975 at a cost of more than £9m. Thus, the Irish Distillers Group comprises one of the world's newest distillery plants, and certainly the world's oldest licensed whiskey distillery currently in production.

From the outset the priorities for *Old Bushmills* were clear. They were — to develop and to modernise it, to increase the output and to bring to it all the professional marketing skills that were necessary. The aim was to make it a first-class and a self-sufficient distillery in its own right. And to that end some £4-5 millions were invested.

Crucial

The man chosen to go to the North for the crucial job of expansion and the equally crucial diplomacy required for such a delicate public relations exercise was Richard Burrows, who later became managing director of Irish Distillers. Burrows, the son of a noted Irish Times journalist, qualified in Dublin as an accountant. He has the build of a rugby football prop forward — which he has been — and the sure touch of a man who remembers a name and a face, but behind the youthful charm there is more than a hint of the steel required for such a tough and demanding job.

He remembers his early days at Bushmills. "It seemed in need of great improvement, though it had the tremendous charm and character which it retains today. There was also the need for a greater sense of urgency, for more thrust and more drive and for more money to be put behind the brand. It is important to stress that morale was good. The people there are very quick, and it took most of them about 25 seconds to size up my background!"

"I always got on tremendously well with the *Old Bushmills* people. We never had any industrial relations problems and if they were asked to come in and work harder or longer there was a great feeling of involvement, to meet delivery times and to get orders away. They were really good workers."

Light-hearted

There were lighthearted memories too and these included the story of the goat. "I am a dreadful gardener and our house at Castlerock had far too much lawn for my liking. One of the boys at the Distillery suggested that I buy a goat to keep down the grass. So we bought a beast which was promptly named Daisy May. The idea was to

One of the major developments of the mid-Seventies was the expansion of the Distillery. This picture shows the erection of new warehousing, with the main Distillery Buildings in the background.

tether her on a long rope and let her eat so much grass every day. I soon discovered that the last thing a goat will eat is grass. Even if she is dying on her knees! So, as you can guess, it was me who was sent out in all weathers, day and night, to look after this damned goat. It didn't do much for the grass, but it was all part of the fun of being at *Old Bushmills.*"

One of the major developments during Burrows' period as managing director was the expansion of the Distillery. He relates one of the "inside" stories, with typical panache. "I had made arrangements for a bank loan of some £1.5 millions, which seemed a great deal of money, to a young man of only 26. I attended our Board Meeting and I was not a little nervous, in the circumstances. They called me in, and I outlined the plan. It went through 'on the nod', and that was that!"

Right course

During his four years at *Old Bushmills,* Richard Burrows set the company on the right course. Its own Board was established with Sir William Jenkins as chairman. Sir William had made his fortune in India and returned to his native Ulster to enter public life and to hold a clutch of important directorships in the business life of the local community. He was also a former Lord Mayor of Belfast and in that office he acted with considerable political vision and courage. Members of the original Board also included Clem Ryan, former production director of Irish Distillers, and Michael Gibson, the Belfast solicitor, who made his name much further afield as one of the greatest Irish international rugby players of all time.

Richard Burrows returned to Dublin to take up a senior position in 1976, and two years later he succeeded Kevin McCourt as managing director of the Irish Distillers Group.

Meanwhile *Old Bushmills* continued to flourish and Richard Burrows' successor was Bill McCourt (no relation to Kevin McCourt). Bill was born in the United States but returned with his parents to Belfast at an early age and later carved for himself a notable career in local industry. His father, an Ulsterman, settled in New York with his Dublin-born wife , and spent many years there as the local representative of a Belfast textile firm. Bill McCourt says "I was there until I was nine, and I loved New York and the atmosphere of the place. I still have a great natural affinity for the United States. I strongly believe that the place where you are born and bred forges a link which you never lose. We now have so many connections with North America that I immediately feel at home in that country."

Back in Belfast the young Bill McCourt decided to follow his father into the textile business. He joined the York Street Flax Company and began a four-year Diploma course in textile technology. The company, around that time, decided to employ a firm of outside business consultants and Bill McCourt was seconded to them. "That was extremely important for me" he says "I was able to detach myself from my company and to work with a group of people who had a wide experience in all aspects of industry.' Later he took a Diploma in Industrial Management and joined another large textile firm, working as an internal consultant.

Sir William Jenkins
former chairman

George Cameron
former chairman

Charles Neill
chairman of "Old Bushmills"

Richard Burrows (left) managing director of the Irish Distillers Group, and a former managing director of "Old Bushmills". On the right is Bill McCourt, the current managing director of "Old Bushmills".

He then had the opportunity to join an engineering company. "To me it is the most challenging of all forms of industrial organization. I felt that if you could master engineering then most other tasks would fall in line.' And so it proved. The giant Rolls-Royce Aero Engine organization decided to open a plant in Belfast and McCourt joined that company as its personnel and administration manager. "Initially I had responsibility over matters concerning people, but was later appointed Deputy General Manager before taking over the top post a couple of years later."

Skill

The company was making components for the complete range of Rolls-Royce aero engines. But then disaster struck. There was a scarcity of work in the group and three peripheral factories, including the Belfast plant, were to be run down. In human terms it was the beginning of the blight of recession and unemployment that was to scar the face of the industrial landscape for so long. In managerial terms it required a great deal of planning and skill to maintain a plant and at the same time to run it down gradually. Quite often a person's best qualities are seen in adversity, and it was these qualities that helped to impress Irish Distillers when Bill McCourt applied successfully for the job as managing director of *Old Bushmills*.

His tenure of office has been characterised by a further streamlining of production techniques and a firm commitment to a strong public image, as befits his

Members of the Board under the chairmanship of Sir William Jenkins included Michael Gibson (left), a Belfast solicitor who was also one of the greatest players to wear an Irish rugby jersey; and Clem Ryan, a director of Irish Distillers.

outgoing personality. "The pressure during my last days at Rolls-Royce stood me in good stead, although I was only to see that clearly with hindsight. The big challenge was to get on top of production and distribution at *Old Bushmills*. In the next six years we doubled production capacity and with only a small increase in staff. My job has been to secure an adequate supply of the highest quality whiskey while at the same time ensure that *Old Bushmills* remains a profit orientated organisation. With these ingredients we can look toward the future with every confidence.

Bill McCourt is not the type of man to claim sole credit and he points consistently to a team effort, not least from former chairman George Cameron, a distinguished Ballymena-born accountant, and the present chairman Mr. Charles Neill a well-known Belfast businessman. George Cameron was instrumental in continuing the role of his predecessor and in helping to give *Old Bushmills* a feeling of its own autonomy and Northern identity within the larger group. He tells with relish the story about his tour of the Distillery. He asked a member of senior management about the ratio of malt whiskey in "Black Bush". He was told firmly and politely; "Mr. Cameron, there are some things even a Chairman cannot know!"

Farewell from Donegall Quay in Belfast as yet another emigrant ship sets sail for the New World. This painting is by James Glen Wilson, 1827-63 (Ulster Museum collection). In the 18th Century some 250,000 Ulster people left for North America. There was a second exodus in the 19th Century when around four million Irish emigrants, many of them from Ulster, crossed the Atlantic. The Irish made a distinctive contribution to the land that gave them opportunity and hope.

the prosperity I have had in business since my commencement on the 1st of March. I rented a store and dwelling at the corner of Broad and Bedford (Streets) and have commenced a rectifying distillery and liquor store, and at that business I appear to be getting along very well. The store I have rented for 150 dollars per annum.''[8]

Emigration had a particular significance for the liquor trade. It not only increased the potential markets abroad, but it introduced old skills to a new continent. John Ed Pearce in his history of one of America's major distillers, Brown-Forman of Kentucky, states; ''Germans, Irish and Scots moving into western Pennsylvania brought the art of distilling with them, and when they pushed down the Monongahela and Ohio, it went along. A remote farmer might have trouble hauling 20 bulky bushels of grain to town to exchange for nails, cloth, salt and tools, but a single horse could carry the 40 gallons of whisky the 20 bushels would yield, and the whisky would bring more. Small wonder that 25 years after Kentucky was settled there were 2,000 registered, and goodness knows how many unregistered, stills.''[9]

Interestingly, a second cousin to a founder of Brown-Forman came from a townland near Londonderry in Ulster, not far from *Old Bushmills*. James Thompson arrived in Louisville in the latter part of the 19th century to begin a career that would establish a prominent Kentucky whisky name. When a descendant of the first Browns decided to build a summer house in 1911 it was called 'Avish' — the name of the ancestral home near Londonderry from which the young James Thompson had ventured out in 1875. Much later, by a series of fortuitous circumstances, the Brown-Forman Corporation acquired rights to market *Old Bushmills* in the United States, thus strengthening the links between Ulster and Kentucky that had been already established, long ago.

Exports

The steady emigration of the 18th and 19th centuries opened many new markets for Irish whiskey, and Irish distillers exported to those countries to which the settlers had found their way. *Old Bushmills* advertised not only in publications in India, but also in South Africa and the Middle East, as well as in the United States.

Irish whiskey gained a formidable reputation in America during these years, and *Old Bushmills* won gold medals at the Chicago World's Fair in 1893, and the St. Louis World's Fair in 1904, when Irish whiskey was promoted and sold at ''five cents a paralyzing glass!'' Before Prohibition, ''Irish'' was synonymous with good whiskey but later its reputation was damaged by bootleggers who put Irish labels on their ''rotgut'' spirits to imply that they had quality. Whiskey from Ireland took a long time to regain its earlier status in the U.S.

The Prohibition on the manufacture, transportation and sale of alcohol in America became law in 1920, but during the next 13 years Americans learned the hard way that, whatever had been and were the abuses of alcohol, legislation alone could not instil moral fervour into a nation if enough people had contrary ideas.

"Old Bushmills" gained a formidable reputation not only in America, where it won gold medals at Chicago in 1893 and St. Louis in 1904, but also in Europe and nearer home. It struck gold in Paris in 1886, 1889 and 1900, in Cork in 1883, Liverpool in 1886 and London 1895. "Old Bushmills" also took top honours in Adelaide in 1887, and it won the Franco-British Gold Medal in 1908.

And contrary ideas they had! Prohibition led to all kinds of unsavoury practices. John Ed Pearce outlines some of these;

> ". . . Prohibition's failure on such a magnificent scale made its repeal inevitable. Not only were Americans drinking more than in pre-prohibition days, they were drinking worse. Thousands were blinded and other thousands crippled with 'jake leg' because of poison Jamaica ginger used in 'bathtub gin'. The public attached glamour to the gangsters who furnished the thirsty country with beer and liquor. The sympathy of the public was more often with the mountain moonshiner than with the judge who regularly — and futilely — sent him off to prison.
>
> "In towns large and small, men who could afford it had their own bootleggers, and boasted of the quality of their wares in contrast to the offerings of the furtive moonshiners who coloured their 'white lightning' with cow manure or iodine, flavoured it with tobacco or dumped carbide into the barrel to give the resulting whisky a 'bead'. The illicit trade finally became so open that bootleggers in New York City distributed handbills in apartment houses containing price lists and the bootlegger's telephone number."

"Curiously, considering the aim of prohibitionists to end all drinking, the dry era actually increased consumption and created whole new classes of drinkers. Prior to prohibition, the average working man was a beer drinker, who stopped by the corner saloon for a schooner of lager on his way home in the evening, and reserved whisky for special formal or festive occasions. Women, too, seldom drank whisky — at least not in public. But prohibition changed this. The blue-collar worker could choose only between the pocket bootlegger or the noisy speakeasy, and could not always afford the speakeasy. And in the speakeasy a generation of college girls learned to drink hard liquor not only because it was available, but because it had become the thing to do. It would take American drinking habits a long time to recover. Many stomachs never would."

"By 1932, the people clearly had had enough. Herbert Hoover clung to his insistence that prohibition could work. Franklin D. Roosevelt promised repeal and a New Deal. The moment he was elected, the distillers started making plans."[10]

Shrewd

Across the Atlantic shrewd businessmen in the liquor trade had been making plans as well. One of these was Wilson Boyd, who had just taken over the *Old Bushmills* Distillery on the death of his father. As soon as Prohibition ended, Boyd was on his way to America to consolidate his own "new deal". Not surprisingly he did extremely well. He had a first-class product, and he had the initiative and business flair that fitted exactly the America of the day.

On Boyd's return from the United States, there were glowing reports in the local newspapers. The "Belfast Telegraph" of November 30, 1933 stated; "A large-scale shipment of whiskey from Ulster, described as the first since the repeal movement in the United States, is to take place from Belfast to New York tomorrow. The Old Bushmills Distillery Company has received a permit for the liquor and the United States Consulate in Belfast is making all arrangements to facilitate the export.

"We are delighted to get the order" Mr. S. Wilson Boyd, the head of The Old Bushmills Distillery Company, told a 'Telegraph' representative. "The whiskey is to be sent direct to New York and all the necessary licences are in our possession for the shipment. It is the only order, so far as I can find out, to be completed under official permit. We regard it as a great compliment to our firm and it is some recognition of our efforts to secure orders in America. We hope the order is the forerunner of many others."

His hopes were indeed fulfilled. Twelve days later the 'Telegraph' announced "Another Large Order", and reported the news thus; "Yet another order for whiskey from the United States reached Belfast today. This was received by The Old Bushmills Distillery Company, and it creates a record in many respects. Mr. S. Wilson Boyd, the head of the firm, said that many thousands of cases were involved. "It is probably one of the biggest shipments of bottled whiskey that has ever left Ireland" he added. "It is unlikely to be completed before Christmas and entails a

The ending of Prohibition in the U.S.A. in 1933 provided great business opportunities for "Old Bushmills", which had been stocking up in preparation for America going 'wet' for more than ten years!

great amount of extra work for our staff and the Customs men. The whiskey is for New York, Chicago and San Francisco."

More than a week later the "Telegraph" reported yet further developments. "There has been a remarkable sequel to the receipt of large whiskey orders in Belfast from America. Whitehall has agreed to the Customs men working overtime, which means that bonded stores in Belfast remain open to enable the consignments to be forwarded promptly. Staff start early each morning and work late at night to cope with the rush orders, which involve a very substantial amount of money." However, Wilson Boyd reassured the newspaper's readers that there were still ample supplies for the home market, and in doing so he neatly summarised his company's wealth of resources and also his own commercial foresight. "My firm has huge stocks, approximately 18 years supply, in bond, even if we never made another gallon. Besides, we have been preparing for America going wet for more than ten years!"

With that kind of impetus, *Old Bushmills* was set fair to weather the commercial storms of the Thirties, but the advent of the Second World War cast a shadow over the Irish distilling industry. In the South the Government in Dublin imposed quotas on exports to maintain sufficient supplies for the home markets. In the North, part of the *Old Bushmills* export quota was kept for the off-duty refreshment of the thousands of U.S. Servicemen, who trained in Ulster in preparation for the fierce fighting during the invasion of Europe. The War also severely curtailed the production of whiskey at *Old Bushmills* because grain was needed for food supplied. But the Distillery survived and its network of outlets at home and abroad had been firmly enough eatablished to withstand the trauma of war.

This was due in no small way to the initiative of Wilson Boyd, particularly with regard to the American market where supplies were handled by Alex D. Shaw and Company of New York, and later by the National Distillers' Corporation. At the end of the Second World War, the Boyd family of Belfast sold out to British businessman Isaac Wolfson, who had made his name in the textile trade.

This advertisement from the Overseas Daily Mail of December 23rd, 1933 showed that "Old Bushmills" knew exactly how to make the best of a golden opportunity.

Colourful

Around this time yet another colourful character entered the long story of *Old Bushmills* — Colonel Henry C. Kaplan, a friend of Wolfson and a New York entrepreneur whose own background was part of the legend and romance of the penniless emigrant who found fulfilment and riches in America, the land of opportunity.

Kaplan was born in Chelsea, Massachusetts. His parents had grown up in Czarist Russia, and life was extremely difficult for members of the Jewish community. His father was an orthodox rabbi, and towards the end of the 19th century the economic and other prospects were so bleak that the parents moved to the United States. They settled in Massachusetts, where Henry Kaplan's parents, his two brothers and sister, and his half-brother, learned all about the rigours of economic survival.

The boys took whatever chores they could find to eke out the meagre family budget. Yet even at an early age Henry Kaplan was demonstrating the brilliant flair for salesmanship that later characterised his business career. He was awarded a medal for selling more copies of the "Saturday Evening Post" than any other ten-year-old in America!

The family went into the molasses business and with their considerable commercial acumen, and sheer hard work, they prospered. In the years before Prohibition was repealed, Henry Kaplan was a member of the New York Stock

A major figure in the "Old Bushmills" story in America was Colonel Henry Kaplan. His own background was part of the legend and romance of the penniless immigrant who found fulfilment and riches. He is pictured here in Army uniform. He served with the U.S. Corps of Engineers in India, during the Second World War.

Exchange. After the restrictions were lifted, he went into the beverage trade and he was President of Oldetyme Distillers Inc., where he developed such brands as Three Feathers and Green River blends. Then in 1940 he sold Oldtyme to the Schenley Distillers' Corporation, and became President of the Knickerbocker Liquor Corporation, a Schenley subsidiary.

He left the exotically-named Knickerbocker Corporation during the Second World War and served with the Corps of Engineers in India, where he eventually became a Colonel. He retained this title in civilian life, and his style and flamboyance fitted exactly "The Colonel", as he was known to everyone.

After the war he started another wholesale operation and this continued until 1948 when he formed Quality Importers Inc. His main brands were Ambassador De Luxe Scotch and *Old Bushmills.* He obtained the latter through his friendship with Isaac Wolfson, who at that time owned the Irish distillery.

Kaplan based his major sales drive on the two brands until 1967, when they came under the control of the Brown-Forman Corporation of Louisville, Kentucky. Since then they have been marketed in America by Jos. Garneau Co. of New York, a Brown-Forman subsidiary. When Colonel Kaplan sold Quality Importers, he went to live in Florida, married a young and attractive English woman and spent his retirement touring the world with Mrs. Kaplan.

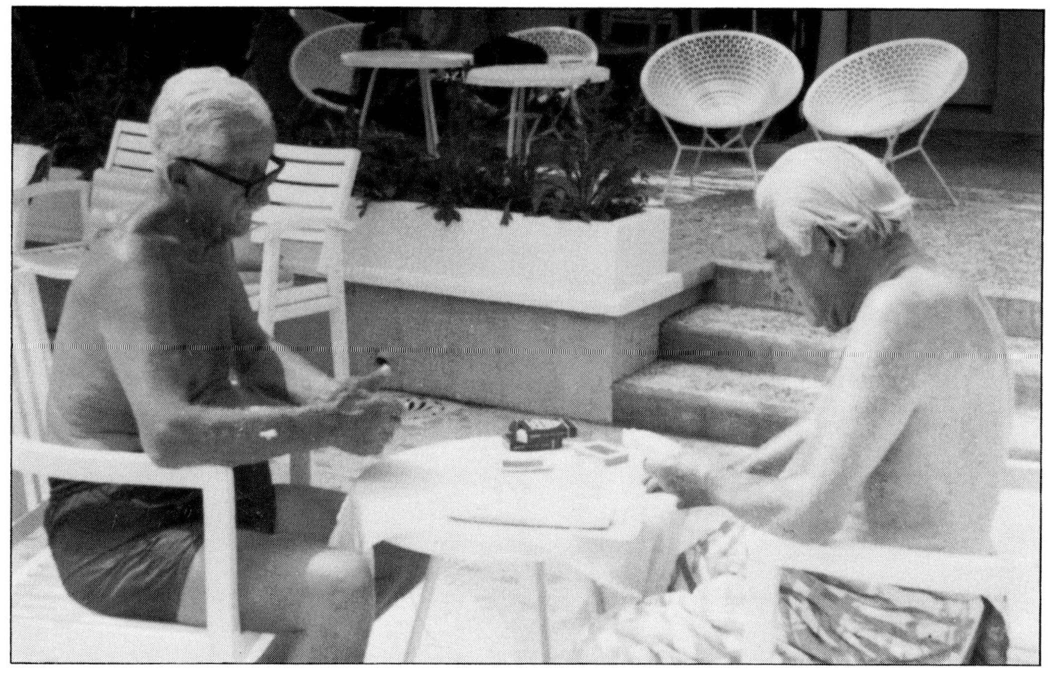

Henry Kaplan (left), playing cards with his old friend Isaac Wolfson in Monte Carlo. At one time Wolfson owned "Old Bushmills" and the American marketing rights were obtained by Kaplan.

Human

Behind this business biography, however, lies the human story of a man of style and generosity who inspired great loyalty and affection among his staff and close associates. In his early Eighties he was living in a health spa at Miami Beach and although he still displayed some of the charm of the old days, a series of bad falls had sapped his strength and dulled his memory. Nevertheless an intimate picture of his business and life-style has been provided by friends in Florida, Kentucky and New York, and by newspaper articles from the America of his heyday.

There is no doubt that he was an outstanding salesman. One business executive in Kentucky noted; "Henry was the kind of guy who could come on the telephone and talk about Ambassador and *Old Bushmills* for a fortnight without stopping!" Another insight into his style is provided by the April 1963 edition of the Kansas Beverage News.

"The brand name that is Colonel Henry C. Kaplan's principal business occupation these days might well be applied to the man himself — Ambassador Deluxe. Colonel Kaplan, a man who lives in the Waldorf Towers in New York and counts among his friends leading civic, business and political figures, can be found any day rubbing elbows with common folk like advertising and newspaper men!"

"He's no ivory-tower executive sitting comfortably on his title of president and chairman of Quality Importers Inc. and letting the others do the work. This came out in a recent luncheon with New York newsman Joseph Kaselow at Al Cooper's

Henry Kaplan was a dynamic salesman who took a deep personal interest in "Old Bushmills". Here the Kansas Beverage News of April, 1963 carries the cover story about this ambassador extraordinary.

on West 36th Street off Herald Square. "Our table was close to the bar and all of a sudden" wrote Kaselow "in the middle of a conversation, the Colonel excused himself and walked over to the bar, got in friendly conversation with two men who were drinking another brand of Scotch, and switched them to Ambassador Deluxe. He can do it, one of the party commented, because he's got a way about him. If you or I tried it, we'd get a fat lip!"

"Another time at Al Cooper's, we were told, he looked up and down the bar, decided there wasn't enough Ambassador Deluxe showing (it was all over the place) bought drinks for the bar, and what's more, left an order for a certain time that night, even though he wasn't going to be there." Kaselow also wrote in the New York Herald Tribune about the occasion when he and Kaplan were lunching in Al Cooper's, and the proprietor mentioned that he was setting off for the Plaza to discuss the catering for a wedding-party.

"Have they decided on their liquor?" the Colonel asked.

"Not that I know of" said Mr. Cooper.

"Well then let's go" the Colonel said.

And he was off to the Plaza on the scent of a sale."

Kaplan also applied great single-mindedness to *Old Bushmills* as the Kansas Beverage News notes; "An energetic sales program has accounted for ever-increasing exposure for this Irish product in the United States, a country — statisticians are quick to point out — that has more of Erin's sons than the old sod itself. The increased preference of so many people for Irish has made *Old Bushmills'* position secure among the Quality Importers brands that are nurtured by Colonel Kaplan."

Legendary

Kaplan's legendary dedication to his own brands — he would drink nothing else — was recalled by his long-time associate Sol Abeles, a New York writer. Typically, as he talked about his old friend, Abeles was dining in the elite "21" Club in Manhattan's West 52nd Street, the haunt not only of film stars, well-known authors, and business and political leaders past and present, but also a favourite rendezvous of Henry Kaplan in his prime.

Abeles remembers; "He took it as a personal affront if any of his close friends ordered anything other than Ambassador Deluxe or *Old Bushmills*. I knew Henry Kaplan for more than 50 years, and for 30 of these he lived in a suite at the Waldorf. I can still remember the number — RS 15. Henry was the greatest salesman I ever knew. One day we were flying from the West Coast to New York but Henry announced suddenly "I'm stopping off at Utah." I asked in surprise "Whatever for?" and Henry said "I don't think they are doing enough in Nebraska." So we took yet another plane to Omaha, and we checked in at a local hotel. Henry asked them to give him flashlamps, and we went round the town in the darkness shining the lamps into the windows to liquor stores to check if Ambassador and *Old Bushmills* were on display. In no time at all the police picked us up and asked what

"The New Yorker" and "Old Bushmills" — a great team over many years.

The Waldorf-Astoria in New York where Henry Kaplan had a suite for 30 years.

the hell we were doing. We had to talk our way out of that one, but that's the kind of salesman Henry was!''

As Abeles reminisced in the rarified atmosphere of the ''21'' Club, with the chic female diners and their escorts, the memories came flooding back of the New York world of Kaplan and his friends. He was a man's man, fond of prize-fighting and horse-racing and he knew all the theatrical people, as well as those in the allied worlds of show-business and entertainment.

''Henry knew everyone, and everyone knew him'' said Abeles. ''All the band leaders like Benny Goodman, the Dorseys, Xavier Cugat, . . . We saw every major fight in New York. Henry would go down to Louisville for the Kentucky Derby and take a box at the track. He was that kind of man. If he won anything, he would more likely or not spend it on the people in his company. He wasn't a big drinker. He drank to be sociable, and he only drank Ambassador Scotch or *Old Bushmills*.''

The elite ''21'' Club in New York, the haunt of the rich and famous, and a favourite rendezvous of Henry Kaplan in his prime.

Abeles travelled abroad with Kaplan on a number of occasions, and they visited *Old Bushmills* as the guests of Wilson Boyd. Abeles again; "The Boyds were lovely, gracious people and they made us feel at home. We found the *Old Bushmills* Distillery to be full of character and, incidentally, with more than its fair share of pretty girls! Henry said to me 'Sol, this place is terrific, but if I owned the distillery it would be going flat-out!' "

Abeles' reminiscences help to create the portrait of a man of the world who was extremely able and generous but who also had an almost innocent charm. "When we travelled I was able to tell him things that he had never heard before, and he was so often astonished. When I pointed out that on Michaelangelo's statue of Moses the cuticles of the nails were absolutely perfect, he marvelled! One time when we were in France I referred in passing to Napoleon's limited formal education, and Henry brightened up considerably — think he felt that there was still hope for him!"

"Above all, Henry was most generous. When we stayed at The Excelsior in Rome he took the smallest room in the suite and left the biggest to me. When we went by train he always took the upper-berth in sleeping-cars. I never met such a considerate human being in my life." Abeles was silent for a while and then a little smile played on his lips as he thought of the old days. He quoted a verse from Burton Braile;

"Thank you for the flowers you sent" she said
"I'm sorry for the words I spoke last night
Your sending flowers proved that you were right,
Forgive me!" — and he forgave her.
And as they talked and walked beneath the bowers
He wondered — who the hell had sent the flowers!"

In the American story of *Old Bushmills* some people had fun along the way.

Tribute

Yet another tribute to Kaplan's business drive and warm human qualities came from Morris Rosen, a former business associate. A lawyer, he worked with Kaplan in New York and remembers the legal details of setting up Quality Imports Inc. in 1948. Rosen also retired to Florida and in a stylish 12th-floor apartment at Miami Beach overlooking Indian Creek and Biscayne Bay he talked about Henry Kaplan and *Old Bushmills*.

"Henry knew me since I was born, because I was directly related to one of his brothers. He had the greatest affection for me since I was a little child. When he was in the Army I attended to some personal matters, but I did not become involved with his business until later. Henry knew everyone in the liquor business. He led the life of a flamboyant bachelor, but he had no hobbies. His hobby was business, and he thought that *Old Bushmills* was one of the best products ever made."

Morris Rosen also visited *Old Bushmills* in Ireland on several occasions and has memories of Wilson Boyd as "a big brusque man and a marvellous person." Rosen was also fond of Belfast. "It was one of the finest cities that I ever visited. In later years I became very sad when I heard what was happening to it."

He also recalled one of the worst sea journeys of his life, from Larne in County Antrim to Stranraer in Scotland. "I thought we were never going to make it. The boat seemed almost to turn over." That journey was made not long after the 1953 disaster when the steamer the Princess Victoria foundered in stormy seas in that same channel, with the loss of 133 lives.

In the main, however, Rosen has warm memories of his visits to Ireland, and he always had a high regard for *Old Bushmills* and Henry Kaplan. "It was not a question of liking the Colonel — I loved him, and that's not a term I use lightly. We also had a special regard for *Old Bushmills*. In the trade it was called 'A little jewel'. It was indeed a quality product for Quality Importers!"

Dynamic

In his business life Kaplan was dynamic, and in his private life he was very much in the social whirl of vibrant New York. But he had another dimension, and this was spotted astutely by Mrs. Janet Boyd, the wife of Austen Boyd. They were Kaplan's guests in New York and also entertained him in Ireland.

She says "In 1963 when my husband travelled on business across Canada we broke our homeward flight in New York and booked in at a small, quiet hotel which was favoured at that time by Belfast people of our acquaintance. When Henry Kaplan heard where we were he insisted that we stay at the Waldorf and he himself booked a room for us, obliging us to pack up and go. The next evening he took us to dinner at one of New York's most elegant and expensive restaurants, 'The Four Seasons'." All of which sounds like the public Henry Kaplan, but she noticed another side to the man.

"He visited Northern Ireland a number of times. He always appeared to be keyed up to a high pitch of enthusiasm about some business deal or other, but he made similar remarks to my son Kenneth and me at separate times, after walking in the garden at our home or looking through the sitting-room window; 'In a place like this I could relax, I could be happy'."

That inner wistfulness and privacy was a quality mentioned more than once by Henry Kaplan's wife Sallye. "He liked to cultivate the image of being a ladies' man, but deep down he was shy. Essentially he was a private person, sensitive and very kind." Their own story has a great deal of romance. Sallye was born in England and

The eye-catching American advertising campaigns in the story of "Old Bushmills" had their own distinct appeal.
On this page the glasses depict various interests. Included are yachting, writing and music.

Opposite are other examples of advertisements during the last quarter-century.

Old Bushmills.
It's changing people's minds about Irish Whiskey.
IMPORTED
FROM THE WORLD'S OLDEST DISTILLERY
OLD BUSHMILLS
IRISH WHISKEY
ORIGINAL GRANT 1608
Experience the taste that experience created. Old Bushmills. Since 1608.

OLD BUSHMILLS
IRISH WHISKEY
Where do you think whiskey came from in the first place?
Ireland? Exactly. The very word whiskey comes from the old Irish "Uisge Beatha" — water of life.
We're not sure when the word about whiskey got out.
It may have been in the second century, when Cairbre Riada and his fellow Scots (as they were called then) left the Bushmills country of Ireland. Cairbre and his band sailed east across the sea and settled in a land to become known as Scotland. You've heard of it. Maybe you've even heard of their whisky.
Or the word may not have got out until the 12th century when England invaded Ireland and found the distillation of spirits to be a local, thriving art. This form of art was something quite new to the British and they became very interested in it.
No matter. The significant thing is that the secret has been out for some time now and nobody has come up with that Old Bushmills flavor yet. To put it in words. Old Bushmills has that burnished scotch flavor without burnished scotch heaviness, that blended whiskey smoothness without blended whiskey blandness.
But enough of this. Knowing history won't help you enjoy Old Bushmills. You enjoy Old Bushmills by putting it in your favorite drink. Every drop is bottled in Ireland. Every drop is 9 years old. Every drop comes from the oldest distillery in the world.

Bushmills.
The whiskey that spans the generations gap.
For 300 years, a whiskey from Bushmills has been with us. 15 generations, fathers and sons, have refined it. The result: Near perfection. Bushmills. Full of character. But not heavy-handed about it. Flavorful. But never overpowering.
Bushmills is unique. Reflecting the past beguilingly, with a light and lively flavor that is all today.
Compare it to your present whiskey. One sip at your favorite pub will tell you why Bushmills has intrigued so many generations. It is, simply, out of sight.
IMPORTED
BUSHMILLS
FROM THE WORLD'S OLDEST DISTILLERY

OLD BUSHMILLS DISTILLERY
WHAT WE HAVE LOVED FOR CENTURIES, YOU WILL LOVE IN SECONDS.
Since 1608 it's been the same old story.
People love Old Bushmills the second they taste it.
Because Old Bushmills is smooth and mellow. A smoothness not easily come by.
The secret lies in an ancient process that goes back centuries to Ireland. To the village of Bushmills, and the oldest whiskey distillery in the world.
Here we pick the local barley ripe for harvest in nearby fields.
We draw clear water from the River Bush, water born for whiskey.
We commit these and other choice ingredients to our age-old triple distillation process.
Then our whiskey matures in handmade oaken casks.
When it finally comes of age years later, only then is it worthy of our label.
Old Bushmills.
But, like 18 generations before you, you'll know exactly what that means.
After your very first taste.
OLD BUSHMILLS
The taste you don't have to acquire.

Charm

Street can be slightly formal at first but he soon mellows and there is a hint of the youthful charm and the steel behind the surface that is not unlike that of Richard Burrows, the Managing Director of the Irish Distillers Group, and the former Managing Director of *Old Bushmills*. It was no surprise perhaps that the two became personal friends and it is certainly no accident that the profile of *Old Bushmills* in America soared when each was at the helm of the distribution company and the producers respectively.

This friendship was cemented whether in Ireland when Street visited *Old Bushmills* and endured the morning after, as much as he had enjoyed the day before, or when Burrows and Street met in California where *Old Bushmills* sponsored a series of highly-successful powerboat races. It should be emphasized, however, that the American regard for *Old Bushmills* is not based on friendship or sentiment alone. The Brown-Forman philosophy, so well enunciated by Dan Street, has not changed; "This is a bottom-line company" — in other words the main consideration at the end of the day is that the bottom line on the financial report shows a profit.

This applies as much to *Old Bushmills* as to all the other Brown-Forman brands, many of them world famous including Southern Comfort, Jack Daniels, Old Forester and Early Times Bourbon Whisky. Ironically, however, the purchase of *Old Bushmills* from Colonel Kaplan's Quality Importers in 1967 was something of an afterthought. Bill Street explained "Kaplan had several brands but the two most important were Ambassador and *Old Bushmills*. However Brown-Forman had been

For several years "Old Bushmills" sponsored a series of highly-successful powerboat races in California.

looking for the right type of Scotch to add to the portfolio. We had our eyes on Ambassador which had a strong base in New York and we hoped to get it based throughout the country. That was one of the main reasons for buying Quality Importers but we realised very soon that we also had a 'little jewel' in *Old Bushmills.* It had the finest quality, an attractive look about the bottle, and a great romance and tradition about its history. And as we continued to visit *Old Bushmills* we got to know the people.

"It ought to be said, however, that one of the key figures in the *Old Bushmills* story on this side of the Atlantic was Harold Halpern who had been one of Kaplan's right-hand men and who stayed on with Garneau. He always had this 'thing' about *Old Bushmills,* like his own little love affair in the company, and it was Harold who impressed on me that we had indeed this 'little jewel' in our possession. He deserves a great deal of credit for the success of *Old Bushmills* in the U.S. It still has big hurdles to cross, but personally I feel that it has a strong future in this country. It will take time, maybe two decades or more, but it could be among the fifty top brands in the U.S., and that would be some achievement."

Under the corporate control of Brown-Forman the "Old Bushmills" label is in the best of company, including "Jack Daniels" and "Southern Comfort". All three are part of the extensive Brown-Forman portfolio.

Granville Nugent is a craftsman who has been producing malted barley for "Old Bushmills" for more than half-a-century. He has made a life-long study of the subject and he can talk about barley from 9,000 BC to the quality of the latest crop on the Ards Peninsula! His father was managing director of McConnells Brewery which was built in Belfast in 1894. His grandfather (pictured here in Belfast) became managing director of J and J McConnell, a local firm of whiskey blenders and wine and spirit merchants. Granville Nugent reflects; "It is staggering to think that I once conversed with a man who was born just twelve years after the battle of Waterloo!"

CHAPTER EIGHT

"John Barleycorn"

On December 22, 1934 the Northern Constitution published a letter from Mr. J. W. Morrison, the manager of the *Old Bushmills* Distillery. It had nothing to do with Christmas or Yuletide spirits, but was concerned with the much more earthy matter of offering advice to local farmers about the barley crop. The quality of this was and still is of vital importance to the Distillery.

James Watt Morrison wrote; "The local price of barley has reached the price of £7-5s a ton. May we draw your farming readers' attention to a few points which we know would, without doubt, further increase the value of barley grown locally — by locally we mean this north-east part of Ireland.

"In the first place any soil will not grow barley any year. In a moderate, dry year heavy ground inclined to clay would produce a nice profitable crop of clear-skinned grain, but on the average it takes fairly sharp soil to produce almost without fail a uniform crop. It has been proved in more countries than this that barley does best as a crop following a root crop, both to the farmer and the consumer.

"Secondly, the quality of the seed should be the best obtainable, and subsequent crops for about three years should keep up to standard. Barley should not be rolled until well brearded, when the grasses may be sown and rolled in. This latter hint is for farmers whose land is heavy, with little or no fear of drought. Next we come to harvesting of the crop, and it is here that a goodly sum is lost. Barley must be dead ripe before cutting; unlike oats, it is impossible to ripen barley in the stook. Furthermore when the grain is properly ripened three good days in stook is sufficient in most cases to root-dry the sheaves, when it can be laid into rickles or huts, or, better still, small stacks of about 12 feet, provided bosses are used and an air vent left at the base.

Moisture

"The length of time the grain may be left in stack is governed by the depth of the farmer's pocket, but here we may give a few figures.

"Normally, harvested barley should contain 12-14 per cent of moisture, the longer in stack the more uniform the moisture and smaller percentage with subsequent higher price for grain. It is our experience that barley grown locally invariably contains 18-22 p.c. of moisture, and we, of course, make ample allowance for this when making our purchases."

"We now come to the threshing operations. Again many lackadaisical samples come on the market, namely, unequal grain, grains showing second growth, weed seeds of various kinds, and grains showing the result of heating in the stacks. It is to prevent this latter fault that bosses and vents are used. Any of the foregoing can be eliminated if a good threshing plant is used and the man in charge of the plant knows his work. In conclusion, barley will raise a higher price if put on the market a pale, golden yellow, clear skinned and dry and showing a little fawn. Closely dressed grain to raise the weight per bushel is not admired nor sought after, especially by maltsters."

The technical language of the letter is now dated, but its sentiments are not. Harvesting has moved from the days of "stooks" and "stacks". Modern technology has largely reduced this traditional skill to the scarcity of a dying art. What remains timeless, however, is the craftsmanship that has been involved in the making of whiskey at every stage of its detailed, precise and yet essentially mysterious process. This has always been a skill closely allied to nature.

The craftsmen who make whiskey have long had an eye for the seasons; for the rain, wind and weather; for the touch of sunshine on the ripening grain; and for the importance of a good harvest. They have been men close to the soil. They know that barley is not just another commodity — it is a living plant. These are craftsmen like Granville Nugent, an Ulsterman who has been producing malted barley for *Old Bushmills* for more than half-a-century, and Willie MacKay, a Scot, who has been making *Old Bushmills* whiskey for well over a decade. Each in his way retains a profound respect for his craft that has changed little for hundreds of years, despite technological evolution.

Blenders

Granville Nugent's long association with *Old Bushmills* began through his father who was managing director of McConnell's Brewery in Belfast which was built in 1894. The address in the early days was Lagan Village — later Ravenhill Road — which is a reminder of the essentially rural aspects of the city in those times. His association with the licensed trade goes back even further. His grandfather James Nugent joined J. & J. McConnell, a Belfast firm of whiskey blenders and wine and spirit merchants, in 1867 and later he became managing director. Granville Nugent says, "I remember him taking me by the hand, and later feeding him in bed shortly before he died. He was a very pleasant and amiable old gentleman. It is staggering to think that I once conversed with a man who was born in 1827, just twelve years after the battle of Waterloo!"

Granville's father — Chester Nugent — obtained a contract in the 1920's to make malt for the Guinness Co. in Dublin. During the Twenties business in the trade was poor and McConnell's brewery eventually went into voluntary liquidation in 1928-1929. Chester Nugent retained his contract with Guinness but he needed

Strangford Lough — an area of great natural beauty and one of the outstanding regions for natural conservation in the British Isles. Men in the malting business have an eye for nature, and the return of the Brent Geese to Strangford marks another shift in the cycle of the seasons and the gathering of a good harvest.

premises for malting. He eventually obtained an introduction to Samuel Wilson Boyd and discovered that *Old Bushmills* had spare malting capacity. So he began to use part of their premises, and later when Wilson Boyd bought the Distillery at Coleraine, the Nugent family used part of these buildings as well.

They were continually producing malted barley under contract for *Old Bushmills* and Guinness and it became obvious that they would need to establish their own independent base, sooner or later. So just before the Second World War the Nugents built their own maltings outside Newtownards and on the edge of Strangford Lough, one of the great areas of natural conservation in the British Isles. Chester Nugent became chairman of the Ards Malting Co. Ltd., and Granville who had joined his father in the business at the age of 19 became managing director. He held this post for 41 years until the company was bought in 1980 by Belfast Warehouses Limited. Granville Nugent remained on the Board as Managing Director and maintained his remarkably long connection with the industry. By the end of 1982 he had spent some 57 years in malting, and 43 of these operating from the same office with its splendid views of the striking beauties of Strangford Lough.

During his career he made a lifelong study of barley. "There are records of barley going back to 9,000 BC, and in 1922 when they opened the Tomb of Tutankhamun who died in 1352 BC they found barleycorn which later germinated when it was soaked in water.

Every jug tells its own story! This container advertising the virtues of "Old Bushmills" Male (and not malt) Whiskey is thought to have come from Czechoslovakia many years ago. It used to have pride of place in a Newtownards licensed premises, but it now sits appropriately in the Potstill Bar at "Old Bushmills".

Arctic

"Man can grow barley in the Arctic region where the soil seldom thaws more than three inches below the surface. It grows on tropical plains, in India, around the Nile Delta where the salt water is seldom more than a foot below the surface, it is grown in the Himalayas at a height of some 15,000 feet, it grows all over Europe, and in Australia, Latin-America and countless other places. The first barley that was ever grown in America was brought over by Christopher Columbus. Barley is the most important cereal in the economy of mankind."

The malting of barley is an art in itself, but — as J. W. Morrison was at pains to point out in his letter of 1934 — it is important that the farmer provides the maltster with good barley. Ards Malting Company has won numerous awards and silver medals for the quality of its produce, and in 1976 it won the Guinness Perpetual Silver Challenge Cup for the best sample of barley grown in Ireland. Granville Nugent explains why the Ards area is so good for producing barley.

"The soil is a light loam, superimposed on a gravelly sub-soil. There is good draining and the relative absence of trees allows as much sun as possible to cover the ground. There is also less variation between day and night temperatures because we are flanked on two sides by salt water — on one side Strangford Lough and on the other the Irish Sea."

The mark of a good maltsman is the appearance of the "floor". There should be no hollows or humps. Turning over the barley requires special skill, almost like handling a scythe. Some of the old-timers had their own designs, and left these on a "piece' of malt, rather like a trade mark.

At Ards they continue to produce malt in the traditional way. Barley is still steeped in water for some 44 hours. Altogether the water is changed four times, and the "last water" is heated to 58 degrees F. to help start the germinating process. The barley itself is turned and aerated mechanically, but staff at the Ards Maltings still use wooden shovels when required. A certain amount of deference is paid to modern technology, but traditional skills and judgement and a "feel" for the product are still of paramount importance.

Granville Nugent says, "It is all very natural, and little has changed in the past 100 years. The production is a little more mechanised and the plant breeders have done a good job in producing strains of barley that are more suited to malting, but the essentials of the business remain the same." The barley produced nowadays by combine harvesters has around 20 p.c. of moisture and this is kiln-dried to reduce the moisture content to some 12 p.c. This is to ensure that barley thus dried will keep indefinitely in large quantities.

"Kiln-drying is one of the most important processes in the maltster's business. If you do your kiln-drying properly the barley will malt, almost in spite of itself!"

Distiller

In simple terms, the whiskey distiller requires starch in quantity to make spirits, and the way to achieve this is by using barley. The job of the maltster is to set free the starch inside the barleycorn. This is contained in tiny granules, and the best way to set the starch free is by controlled germination. The starch is contained in minute cellulose sacs, and during germination the chemicals in the plant change the cellulose to soluble sugar, thus releasing the starch. Granville Nugent notes cautiously "A maltster can over-germinate and under-germinate. It has to be exactly right. It's all a matter of expertise and experience."

Ask him if there is one outstanding quality in a good maltsman, and he will reply — after a long pause — "You require someone who understands Nature. That's the most important quality." By that criterion alone, Granville Nugent knows his malt. He is the kind of man who will notice exactly when the Brent geese return from Scandinavia for the milder winter on Strangford Lough. "In 1982 it was during the night of Sunday, September 12", he says. "That afternoon there wasn't one to be found. The next morning the shoreline was black with them!"

All his life he has been close to the soil. His motto is simple — "Better to roam the fields for health unbought than to fee the doctor's noxious draught." For 22 years he was Master of the Hunt — the North Down Harriers — and even at 75 he enjoyed his daily ride on one of his mounts and looked hardly a day over 65. For 25 years he was Chairman of the Horse Committee of the Royal Ulster Agricultural Society. He was a member of the R.U.A.S. since 1925 and later became Vice-President, President and eventually Vice-Patron. In 1981 he was given Honorary Life Membership of the Royal Dublin Society on its 250th Anniversary. This was awarded to a select few for their service to agriculture, science, industry and the arts. Granville Nugent's citation praised "his outstanding contribution to agriculture in Northern Ireland and his long and dedicated service to the Royal Ulster Agricultural Society."

When a man with this background talks about agriculture his words have a special dimension, and Granville Nugent talks about *Old Bushmills* in this setting. He remembers the Distillery away back in the Twenties.

"There was a time when they used oil lamps, the machinery was driven by a water-wheel which was powered by the little river running through the Distillery, and there were no telephones. I remember when the stills were coal-fired. Somewhere about the place there was a collection of green glass balls which used to hold up a huge anti-submarine net between Rathlin and Fair Head during the First World War".

He also remembers Wilson Boyd — "A likeable man, and a good host" — and the people around the Distillery. "They were always first-class workers and most helpful. Practically all of them had an agricultural background. I have always believed that there is less discontent when people are nearer the land. This is all part of getting back to nature again. I really do think that the closer you are to the soil, the happier you are!"

Roots

Willie MacKay, the Production Director of *Old Bushmills,* is also a man with his roots in the soil. His father was a crofter on the Isle of Skye and he has memories of working close to nature. He says, "I was an only child and I remember having to milk cows, having to use a scythe, and turning the soil with a horse and plough. There were no opportunities in those days to spend school holidays in the Austrian Alps! Later on when my parents fell into ill-health, I had to look after the croft myself."

"It was a valuable experience and it taught me all about hard work. We also did a great deal of fishing in the sea lochs, often from small rowing boats, and mostly for mackerel and whiting or haddock. The food was wholesome and simple — fish and potatoes and home-made bread. There was a steamer service once a week from Glasgow and it used to bring up the oat-meal. We grew our own vegetables and my mother and her sister wove tweed garments. People had to be reasonably self-sufficient. There was always a bottle of whisky in the house, mainly for the cold! The nearest public-house was about 12 miles away. Looking back it was a relatively simple life, but as far as I was concerned it was a good basic start. It gave me a sense of values, and I soon learned that life does not owe you a living."

Willie MacKay was a bright boy and he won a scholarship to Glasgow University — a rare distinction in the early Forties. However his studies were interrupted by the Second World War and he joined the Army. He worked in the Ordnance Corps which gave him valuable experience of office work and later he had a temporary job with the Admiralty. This involved administration in a cash office where 500 men were paid every week.

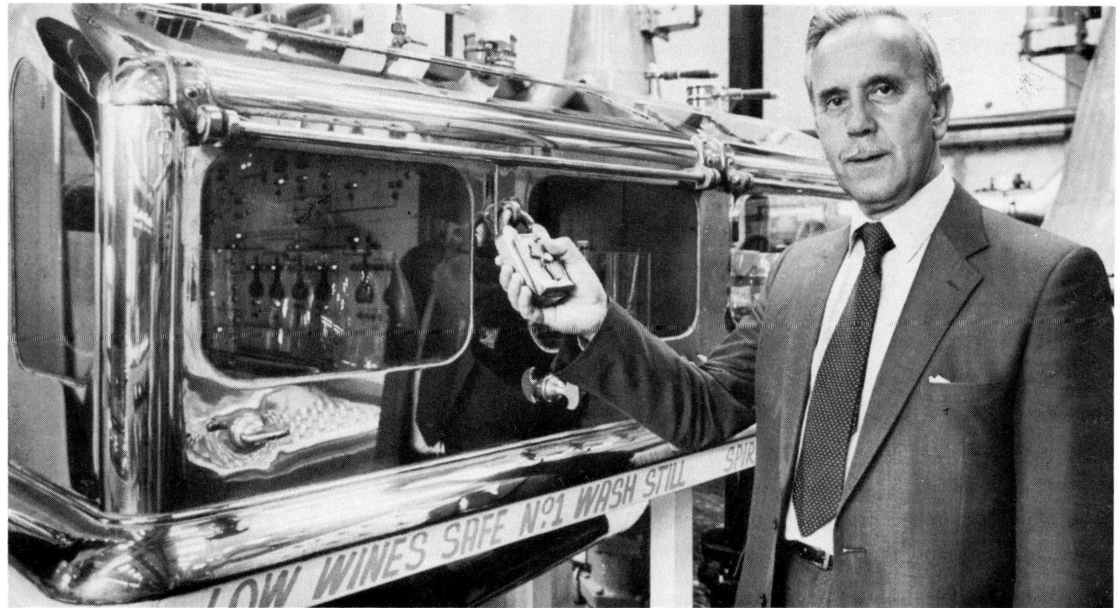

Willie MacKay, the Production Director of "Old Bushmills" has spent a working life in the business, both in Scotland and at Bushmills itself. "In my time there were no formal lectures. You just had to learn it all by practice. Eventually it became a matter of 'feel', of instinct and experience."

This line drawing of the Distillery dates from the late nineteenth century, with — once again — the distinctive Pagoda Towers conspicuously absent.

These drawings, which are part of the one set, show (above) the bonded store in Belfast and (below) the old malting floors at Bushmills.

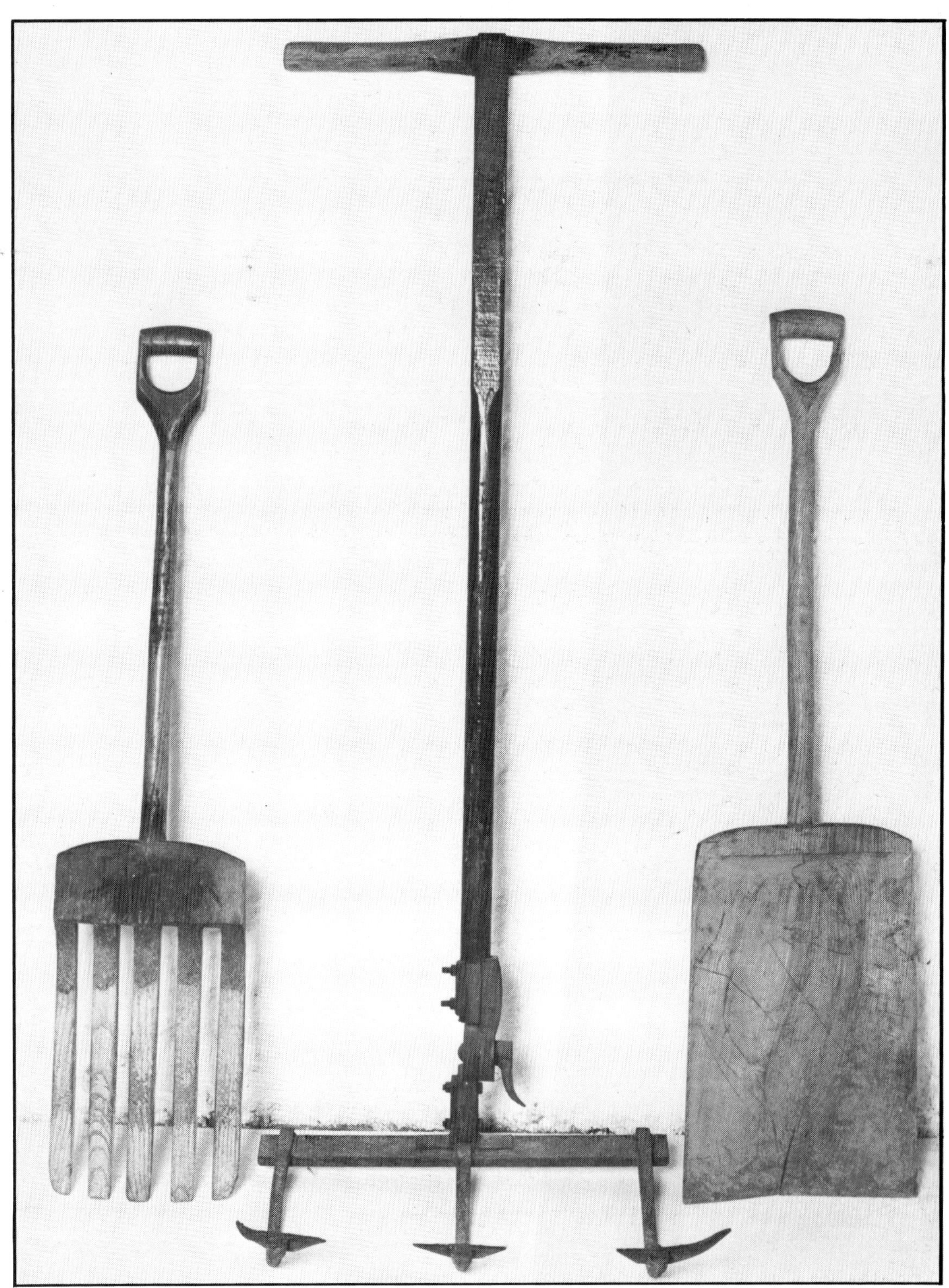

The making of malt in the traditional way required the use of special wooden implements. The barley was turned over to avoid it 'choking' itself by breathing Co2, and the wooden implements were less bruising to the grain than those made from iron.

University

After National Service he had intended to complete his university education and attended the University of Aberdeen but when his parents became ill he had to return to the Isle of Skye. He supplemented his income by taking temporary employment, including that of working with a squad of twelve to unload coal boats. This in turn gave him access to the local Talisker Distillery, some three miles from his home at Carbost. "I was able to go inside and to see what was going on. However, I didn't ask too many questions. It was all a bit secretive!"

Then in one of those twists of Fate, which some regard to be mere coincidence, a vacancy arose when the local clerk in the Distillery was called up for National Service. Willie MacKay was offered the job, and thus began his long career in the whiskey business. He recalls his appointment with a wry smile. "I had been to a Skye wedding, and as you can guess, these were rather long affairs! So the next morning I was not feeling exactly on top of the world when there was a rattle on the window shortly after 7 a.m. The local postman said 'Get up quick, you're going to be interviewed.' So I got out of bed, and I was in the process of feeding the hens when a car drew up. Out stepped the Inspector from the local Distillery, and there was me holding a bucket of hen food!

"However, the interview did not go along the lines I had expected. I was and still am very fond of playing the pipes, and the conversation came round to piping. But I suppose the Inspector was sizing me up in other ways. Anyhow, he reported back to the Distillery and the manager said 'We'll get a lassie to work in the office and we'll take on the laddie as a trainee manager.'

"I had the impression that the Distilleries in the Gaelic-speaking areas wanted managers who could speak the language, and I was fluent in Gaelic. Even today my wife when she wakes up in the morning will ask me the time in Gaelic. It's the first language that comes to her!"

So at the age of 23, Willie MacKay began his apprenticeship in Skye and during the next few years he learned all the practical details of making malt whisky, in the numerous centres where the Scottish Malt Distillers operated.

Stages

"I went through all the various stages — turning the barley in the loft, working as a still man, then on the night shift, then the day shift. It was hard work, but also fascinating. I soon discovered that no two Distilleries were the same. There was a difference in location, environment, local water . . . and all these added up to a different product. There was no strictly organised course, but you were sent to each place to learn from the experts. And you could learn from a good brewer and a good malt-man. In my time there were no formal lectures, you just had to learn it all by practice, and get it all in your head. Eventually it became a matter of 'feel', of instinct and experience."

He still remembers the "characters" and the dedicated craftsmanship of the whisky men. "They were very particular about the way in which they turned over the

The ground malt is mixed with warm water and the mixture is run into a large circular container called a "mash tun." The mixture itself is stirred by huge mechanical forks.

The fermentation creates a reaction as the mixture bubbles furiously like a volcanic spring. The yeast, after some 45 hours, expends itself and the malt sugar has been converted into alcohol. There is an aroma at this stage which is as inexplicable and yet as distinctive as the whiff of whiskey itself.

The ground malt is then mixed with warm water, and the mixture is run into a large circular container called a "mash tun". In Bushmills the "mash tun" is 22 feet across by six feet deep. Into this are poured 10,000 gallons of hot water and eight tons of ground malt. The water (which comes from St. Columb's Rill and is the vital factor in production) is not at boiling point, otherwise it would kill off the diastase. The mixture is stirred by huge mechanical forks attached to the "mash tun" and then left alone for some 45 minutes so that further mixing or "infusing" can take place. The starch in the malt has now become maltose and the resultant liquid is called the "wort".

The "wort" is drained off and piped away for fermentation, and fresh water is run into the large circular container to mix with the residue of the grains that are left. This happens three times, and then the spent grain, known as "draff" is taken away. This used to be sold to dairy farmers but nowadays the spent wash and the spent grain are used in the production of high protein cattle feed. The entire process of making the "mash" is repeated some 21 times a week at *Old Bushmills*.

Malt

The area where this takes place, known as the "mash house", has an atmosphere all its own. The yellow sides of the "mash tun" contrast with the dark red "grist cases" and "hopper" and the stainless steel "underback" and "liquor tanks". The floor is a raised iron grid, and it is definitely not the place for visitors in high heels, though many a trim ankle in stockinged soles has moved nearer the "mash tun" for a peep at the production process. Everything in the "mash house" is kept scrupulously clean, in an area where tradition and technology rest easily side by side.

The "wort" which has been piped from the "mash tun" is now mixed with yeast but it has to be cooled to a temperature at which the yeast, which is susceptible to extremes, can survive. During the fermentation process the yeast reproduces itself at a remarkable rate by feeding on the sugars in the "wort". In so doing it produces a chemical reaction which creates alcohol and Co2. The liquid is fed into another set of large cylindrical containers called "wash backs". It is here that the fermentation takes place and the Co2 is allowed to seep off. In the larger Scottish Distilleries this Co2 is collected and sold commercially.

The fermentation creates a visible chemical reaction as the mixture bubbles furiously like a volcanic spring. There is also a smell as inexplicable and yet as distinctive as the whiff of whiskey itself. Unsuspecting visitors are sometimes asked to smell the droplets of liquid which gather on the large containers, and even the slightest sniff can sting the back of the throat and bring tears to the eyes! After about 45 hours, the yeast has expended itself, and all is silent. The yeast, in simple terms, has converted the malt sugar into alcohol. The wort is now known as "wash" and it is ready for the next stage of distilling. Generally it takes ten gallons of 'wash' to make one gallon of whiskey.

Heated

The wash is then fed into the huge potstills — tall, copper containers with curved necks. The object of distillation is to separate the alcohol in the liquid from the water. The potstill is heated, and the alcohol and water in the form of vapours rise up the curved neck to the condenser, where cold water converts the vapours back into alcohol and water. This is known as "low wines", and each time the liquid is distilled the concentration of alcohol becomes stronger as the water is driven off. The liquid resulting from the second distillation is known as "feints", and the residue is called "spent lees".

In the manufacture of Irish whiskey, distillation takes place a third time — one more than in the production of Scotch. Willie MacKay who has long experience of both, says, "No-one really knows why the traditions of a third distillation grew up, but it does produce a very different liquid." Some people claim that a third distillation removes yet more impurities and that this is one reason why *Old Bushmills* is less likely to create a hangover on the morning after! This would depend greatly on the amount taken, but many regular consumers of *Old Bushmills* would swear by its less painful after-effects, invariably created by excess. The Company, however, cannot advertise that its product is less liable to cause a hangover! Moderation ought not to lead to a hangover at all.

The chemistry of the distilling process is complex, and whiskey men at this stage talk about the "weak" and "strong" portions of the second distillate. The first part of the third distillate is known as the "foreshot". The layman need not worry unduly about such terms. What is important is the fact that the clear liquid which will eventually become *Old Bushmills* whiskey is drawn off during the third process of distilling. The still-man takes a sample and adds a little water. If the liquid turns milky he is still running off "foreshot" and it is not yet ready for the final collection.

Soon afterwards he will try another sample. If after adding water he finds that this liquid stays clear, he is then running off the pure spirit, and at this point he is ready to collect. Willie MacKay explains.

"The still-man then collects the spirit between two predetermined points. It has to have the right balance of flavour. This is not whiskey as such, but the congeners in the liquid give the first flavour to what we eventually call whiskey. The still-man decides at what point the liquid will be just right to help give the final product its characteristic taste. This cut-off point where he collects the spirit is never divulged. This is a trade secret!"

Spirit

This clear liquid is then piped off to a spirit receiver. Technically it cannot be called whiskey until it is three years old, but the production of *Old Bushmills* whiskey takes much longer. This is the story of slow maturation in oak casks and finally the skilful blending by craftsmen. This in itself requires a detailed description

The tall, copper potstills with the curved necks are distinctive features of any distillery. The object of the distillation is to separate the alcohol from the water. In the manufacture of Irish whiskey, distillation takes place three times. "No-one really knows why the tradition grew up, but it produces a very different liquid". The modern potstills are heated by steam, but in the past they were coal-fired.

but it is sufficient at this stage to underline the crucial importance of distilling to produce the precise liquid that will later become *Old Bushmills* and "Black Bush".

The still-room itself looks as if it belongs to the computer age. The huge copper stills are at the heart of the process, the carefully labelled pipes (painted blue for low wines and feints, red for wash, black for spirit and white for water) are like huge tentacles reaching out from the depths of a gleaming engine room. But the focal point is the control deck with its diagrams, and green and red and orange lights. This is the nerve centre of a highly complex technological process, and yet it is comforting to find that the staff who man this control deck need something as old-fashioned as a tin waste-paper basket! As with so much else in the world of distilling, it symbolises the partnership of the old and the new, the fusion of ancient tradition and modern technology.

However it would be misleading to underestimate the sheer volume of production in a modern Distillery like *Old Bushmills* which has the capacity to produce one million gallons of whiskey a year. This requires a consistent production schedule and the most up to date methods of management, and co-operation with the workforce. But whiskey is not produced to a chemical formula alone. It still requires experience, craftsmanship and what whiskey men call the "feel" for the product.

Fine

At every stage it requires fine judgement about the quality of the malt, the exact point at which the distillate should be collected for maturing, and the intricacies of blending after maturing has taken place. Willie MacKay summed up the highly individual characteristics that remain at the heart of a streamlined and multi-million pound business.

"There are all sorts of permutations that will affect the flavour of a whiskey. For example, distillers will not change the individual shape of a still. Then there is the considerable skills required in producing the right distillate and in blending in order to maintain the same continuity of taste over the years. And above all, the quality of the water used in the distilling process is absolutely vital. St. Columb's Rill is the life-blood of the Distillery. But even here the lay-out of the Distillery is important. If we decided to move the Distillery to the other side of the dam we would produce an acceptable whiskey but it might not have the exact flavour of the *Old Bushmills* and the "Black Bush" we make today! That is the whole mystery of making whiskey. It's such an individual thing."

There is no doubt that barley and whiskey, like human beings, do appreciate that special touch . . .

The type of wood and the size of the cask are of crucial importance. Oak is used more than other timbers because it allows the liquid to "breathe." Even the kind of oak itself is important, and experts can tell the difference between oaks from Europe and those from North America. Research has shown also that the size of the cask affects the rate of maturation. A small cask will aid the process because it allows more of the liquid to have contact with the wood.

CHAPTER NINE

"Whiskey Galore"

"A good whiskey has a sweet taste yet mature and rounded. It is something that slides down easily and warms the cockles of the heart!"

This sounds like a quote from the account executive of a top advertising agency who has spent much time and effort in getting the sequence of words exactly right. In fact it is the considered opinion of a man who has been blending Irish whiskey and giving it that special taste for over thirty years. John MacLennan is a craggy and entertaining Ulsterman who is steeped in the history of the *Old Bushmills* Distillery. Like the whiskey he makes, he is rich in character. When he talks about *Old Bushmills* he distils the essence of craftsmanship, flair, intuition and what all whiskey men call "feel".

He lives alone in a bachelor bungalow at Portballintrae, within sight of the Atlantic Ocean with its restlessness and depths and freshness that are not unlike John himself. His conversation is punctuated by deep rolls of laughter, sometimes caustic wit, at other times gentle humour, and always fascinating darts into anything from making whiskey to a detailed knowledge of the American Civil War, or the specific history of the Spanish Armada, or the poetry of William Wordsworth and Wilfred Owen, or the music of George Gershwin and Aaron Copland. John is the kind of man who can say with style "When Ginger Rogers and Fred Astaire stopped dancing I lost interest in the pop scene!"

John's father, like so many others at Bushmills, introduced his son to the world of distilling and whiskey. Donald Leopold William MacLennan was a Scot from Dingwall who left at the age of two when his father, a watchmaker, moved to Roscommon in Ireland and from thence to Letterkenny. John MacLennan, the eldest of three, was born in Burton-on-Trent when his father was a Customs and Excise Officer at a local brewery. Later the family moved to Ireland where he worked in the Customs section at the Lough Swilly Railway. One of the most coveted jobs in the area was that of a Customs and Excise Officer at the *Old Bushmills* Distillery. When such a post became vacant Donald MacLennan grasped his opportunity without delay. "He was always very fond of Bushmills and the Distillery" says John. "And he had a high opinion of *Old Bushmills* whiskey. When it comes to knowing whiskey, Customs men are among the best in the business."

John's mother was an Ulsterwoman, from Fermanagh. "She was a great strong lady who battered away until she was 86."

properly-equipped team and gradually they hauled to the surface a breathtaking treasure. The material thus salvaged was acquired by the Ulster Museum in 1972 at an agreed valuation of £132,000. The Northern Ireland Government contributed a special grant of £88,000 and the rest of the money was raised by public subscription within six months. The Girona treasure is now a major feature in the Ulster Museum).

Incentive

In his book, Stenuit describes how the recovery of the treasure from the sea-bed had been initially frustrating and how he had offered his team a special incentive.

"The season had got off to a rather slow start. The inventories for the end of April and May were not remarkable, lists of fragments, nothing more. The first gold coin, a four escudo piece, did not come up until 11 May. It was Louis who found it. Then in June, Louis had a period of quite incredible luck. While the rest of us would work away staunchly in our corners and after five hours come up with one tiny, badly worn coin, he would be filling his bottomless green bag with a positive ballast of ducats and two-escudo pieces in perfect condition, plus twice as many pieces of eight and a few odd jewels, just for good measure.

"Two miles from Portballintrae, the Irish distil the best whiskey in the world. During the lean days I had made a rash promise and thereby set a precedent; for every ten gold coins I would give the lucky diver a bottle of *Old Bushmills.*

"It must be said that whiskey is as necessary for divers on land as air is under water. It is a well established tradition in Ireland, and I had only been following the example of my predecessor, Sir George Carew, Master of the Ordnance, who used the same device in June 1589 to fire the enthusiasm of his men, when he was trying to raise some Spanish cannon off the West Coast.

"He gives a very good explanation for it in a letter to the Lord Deputy, dated 1 July:

'Yesterday we fastened our haullsers to a cannon of battery or basalyke as we supposed by the length, for they lie four fathoms and a half of water, which was so huge that it broke our cables. Our diver was nearly drowned, but Irish aqua vitae hath such virtue as I hope of his recovery.'

"Irish divers have not lost their faith in the old therapy and it is probably to that that they owe their resistance to the cold. Our friend, John MacLennan, for example, usually dives in a short neoprene suit, with bare arms, bare hands, bare legs and bare feet. Just to look at him, perfectly happy on the sea-bed in such a state of undress, is enough to make one shiver. I must admit, though, he is a special case. John does actually make *Old Bushmills* whiskey . . ."[1]

Subsequently John made a scale model of The Girona and presented it to the Distillery. He says "There is also at the Distillery a cannon-ball of about ten inches diameter. It was from a Cannon Royal, mounted at the front of The Girona. Apparently it had been found lying on the shore in the late 19th century. It was taken to the Distillery by someone who bored a hole through it and used it as a counter-weight to open and close a flue on one of the furnaces! There was not much ceremony in those days."

Relics from the Girona shipwreck form a tangible link with the "Old Bushmills" Distillery. A cannon-ball of some ten inches diameter was found on the North Antrim shore in the late 19th century. It was from a Cannon Royal, mounted at the front of The Girona, and it now rests in the Distillery's Potstill Bar. The scale-model of The Girona was presented to "Old Bushmills" by John MacLennan who often swam over the site of the shipwreck in sub-aqua gear and later became a firm friend of the European experts who eventually hauled the breathtaking treasure to the surface.

Treasure

Even if the staff then had little awareness of a treasure on their own door-step, the *Old Bushmills* of today is keenly aware of another kind of treasure that flows regularly along the trough in the Distillery's blending floor as John MacLennan and his colleagues carry out their delicate task. That job begins, strictly speaking, when the clear, distilled liquid is stored away in casks to mature.

The new spirit that is pumped from the Still Room to the Filling Store has a high alcohol strength. It also contains some coarse flavouring compounds or 'congeners' which cause the spirit to be harsh and fiery to the palate — hence the need for maturation for many years in casks.

Before being filled into the casks the spirit is reduced to the required proof strength by adding water which has been de-ionized; that is, specially treated to remove all minerals which might react adversely with other elements during the maturing process.

The average strength of the clear distillate is 145 degrees proof. The strength of spirit is based on the ratio of absolute alcohol to water in a fixed volume and the term 'proof spirit' relates to a standard of alcoholic content or strength. In olden times spirit was deemed to be of proof strength when it was of sufficient alcoholic content to ignite when mixed with gunpowder.

The new spirit that is pumped from the Still Room to the Filling Store has a high alcohol strength.

More recently, alcohol strength was measured by an instrument called the Sikes Hydrometer which had a scale marked off in degrees. The bottom of the scale — zero degrees — represented pure water while the top of the scale — 175 degrees — represented absolute alcohol, the maximum alcohol strength possible. 100 degrees on the Sikes scale represented proof spirit which was a mixture of alcohol and water containing 57.1 per cent alcohol at 60 degrees Fahrenheit. Thus 70 degrees means that the whiskey is 30 degrees 'under proof'.

But there is now a new form of measurement — the percentage of alcohol by volume. The old 70 degrees proof is now expressed as 40 per cent alcohol by volume which means 40 pc pure alcohol and 60 pc water. Some of the old-timers do not approve. One said "When we talked about filling the casks for maturation with spirit at eleven degrees over proof it had a certain romanticism but the modern equivalent of 63.4 pc of alcohol by volume has a rather cold ring about it!"

Casks

The type of wood and the size of the cask are of crucial importance. Oak is used because, more than other timbers, it allows the liquid to "breathe". Some of the more volatile alcohols evaporate through the pores of the wood, which itself is a

The work of the cooper exhibits one of the traditional skills of the Distillery.

living medium. (This point about wood was underlined by the international guitarist Julian Bream in a recent interview in a British national newspaper. He said "Great instrument makers are a special breed and often a bit eccentric, you know, most probably because they're dealing with the unknown. They're working with a living medium-wood").[2]

So it is with whiskey. The volume of the spirit in the cask decreases as some of the liquid, containing the coarser flavouring compounds, evaporates through the pores of the oak while at the same time air is breathed in. The longer the whiskey is kept in the cask the greater the percentage loss.

Complex

Willie MacKay, the Production Director, is also closely involved in the blending process. He takes up the story; "What happens in the barrel is very complex. The liquid itself reacts with the lignums in the wood and if you leave the whiskey in too long it acquires a woody flavour that is not pleasant. The best period for maturation varies, from one whiskey to another, and no-one knows why. The list of chemicals is as long as your arm, and people are now using terms that never existed in my young day! Even the kind of oak itself is important. Just as the quality of peat can vary from one bog to another, it is the same with oak. Experts can tell the difference in the oaks from Europe and North America. Recently there has been a great deal of research into barrel chemistry. In the old days, people filled whiskey into casks and simply stored them away. Nowadays we know that different cask sizes affect the rate of maturation. A smaller cask will aid the maturation because it allows more of the liquid to have contact with the wood."

At *Old Bushmills* several types of cask are used. The biggest is the Whiskey Butt which holds 110 bulk gallons. These barrels are made from American oak and they are bought second-hand. This is because of the high degree of absorption when new wood is used. Normally the second-hand casks have been used to mature whiskey. The Sherry Butt, as the name implies, has been used for sherry, which impregnates the wood and gives the maturing whiskey spirit its distinctive colour and bouquet or smell. Sherry Butts are largely used for the production of "Black Bush", and on rare occasions for other blends.

Another type of cask is the Hogshead which holds 55 gallons and may also have contained sherry. However the most commonly used cask is now the American Barrel which has already contained maturing bourbon. This cask is smaller than the others, holding 42 gallons, and this further helps maturation. The slight charring on the inside, important in the production of bourbon, gives the Irish Whiskey a special flavour.

More recently another type of cask had appeared on the scene — the dump Hogshead. This is a cask rebuilt from the staves of approximately one and a half American Barrels with new ends, to give a content of about 60 gallons. This type of cask has the advantage of the bourbon 'character' plus making more economical use of warehouse space than the traditional hogshead. Quite simply, its shape is such that greater numbers of this cask can be stacked in the warehouse.

Malt

The casks are kept in the warehouse for several years. The actual number of years is determined by the kind of blend they will eventually make. Legally the spirit cannot be called whiskey until it has been maturing for a minimum of three years, but at *Old Bushmills* the process goes on much longer. Willie MacKay explains: "We keep the malt whiskey used for "Black Bush" in cask for a minimum of eight years whilst the age of the malt used in our other blends varies from five and a half to six years. This is one of the reasons why it costs more to produce "Black Bush."

Both Bushmills whiskeys are a blend of malt and grain. (Malt whiskey is made by distilling malted barley in potstills. Grain whiskey is manufactured from maize or other unmalted cereals in a patent or Coffey still. The latter is akin to the industrial manufacture of alcohol and produces a liquid with only a little flavour or character. The purpose of the grain whiskey is to give the malt an even more subtle flavour). The proportion of malt to grain whiskey in the manufacture of *Old Bushmills* and "Black Bush" remains a trade secret, but there is more malt in the latter. At one time the grain whiskey was produced in Coleraine, but this Distillery was closed in 1978 and the grain whiskey now comes from Midleton in Cork.

At *Old Bushmills* there is an accepted formula for blending and every attempt is made to make sure that the taste is consistent throughout the entire production. But this is not a matter of blending merely by numbers, or following a familiar equation. It is still very much a question of "feel", and this remains the skill of the blender. Willie MacKay describes it thus; "The blender's art comes in selecting the particular type of casks in which the whiskey has been maturing. He is like a composer. He has the formula, but you cannot get it right just by numbers alone, simply because of the individual character of the casks.

"The blender's experience is invaluable in choosing the casks for each blend to give him what he accepts to be the distinctive characteristics of that blend. He knows almost instinctively how to keep it right."

Key Figure

The blender is indeed a key figure. John MacLennan talks about his role. "I take into account the type of the barrel — whether it is a Butt, a Hogshead or an American Barrel. The details stamped on the end are also extremely important — the number of litres inside, and when it was stored away. Just by looking at the figures I can tell whether it was laid down in February or November 1975, and then I check with my records.

The quality of the whiskey depends also on where it has been stacked in the warehouse. It loses both strength and volume during the maturing process. Near the top of the warehouse, where the temperature is hotter, the liquid will retain more of its strength but it will have less volume due to evaporation. Near the bottom, where the temperature is cooler, it will retain more of its volume but less of its strength. To a good blender this kind of calculation is instinctive.

When he has made his choice of casks that will go to make up the blend, John MacLennan draws a sample from a number of these as a random check. He will test it by pouring some of the liquid into a glass and sniffing it. Basically he is looking for confirmation that the whiskey has the desired 'nose' or aroma which he would expect from a particular type and age of cask. He can also tell a great deal by looking at it. But tasting a whiskey, unlike a wine, is not a great guide. Spirit has very different distinguishing characteristics.

When the casks have passed all the checks, the malt whiskey and grain whiskey are then blended together. The blend itself is checked by the Distillery tasting panel made up from the employees who work in different departments and who have been chosen because they happen to possess a keen sense of smell. Each blend is carefully checked and the main purpose is to ensure consistency.

The dozen or so people are not asked whether the whiskey is 'good' or 'bad', but whether or not it is the same as a standard blend sample. From time to time slight differences will be found due mainly to individual cask character.

Any variations are carefully noted and taken into account by the blender. When he makes his final selection of whiskey for bottling he will generally choose so much from a number of blends.

The quality of the whiskey depends partly on where it is stacked in the warehouse. Near the top where the temperature is hotter the liquid will retain more of its strength, but it will have less volume due to evaporation. Near the bottom where the temperature is cooler it will retain more volume but less strength. To a good blender, this type of calculation is instinctive.

"Marrying"

Until recently this new blend was filled back into casks and stored for up to six months to allow the different components to settle with one another. This was aptly described as "marrying", a process by which sometimes very different individuals try to learn to meet and to mature together. But just as the institution of marriage itself has taken on a different dimension in a world where divorce seems to be on the increase, the process of "marrying" in the production of whiskey has also altered.

In the old days, water was added to reduce the blend to near bottling strength prior to marrying. This was so that the water and the malt and grain whiskeys would blend perfectly together. It also helped to overcome the phenomenon of haze or cloudiness which occurred when whiskey was stored in very cold conditions.

Recently, however, a new process called 'Chill Filtration' has allowed the blend to be 'married' without water and for a much shorter time. About two days prior to bottling, the water is added to reduce the whiskey to bottling strength. The whiskey is then chilled to a temperature where the haze formed becomes a deposit which is then filtered off and the whiskey will then retain its brightness under all conditions of temperature.

When the casks have passed all the checks, the malt whiskey and the grain whiskey are then blended together. The manufacture of whiskey has been streamlined by modern technology but it remains the prerogative of human skills, from the distilling right through to the nosing and blending.

The control deck is the nerve-centre of a highly technological process, but it is comforting to find that the staff still use something as old-fashioned as a tin waste-paper basket!

The big advantage of Chill Filtration is that it produces a whiskey of the quality of previous blends but in a shorter time. John MacLennan says, a little ruefully "I don't like to admit that these new-fangled things work better, but this one does!"

Plans are already advanced for a new system of blending and marrying which will use a series of vats rather than the traditional old oak casks. Willie MacKay says "Unfortunately it may take some of the mystique out of blending but it will have the advantage of ensuring continuity and consistency of character and quality of the blends and will make the blender's life rather less difficult. And on a wider scale it will reduce the amount of handling of casks and thereby cut down the sheer drudgery involved in humping barrels about."

It is worth noting also that *Old Bushmills* and "Black Bush" are bottled at the Distillery, which is a rare enough occurance nowadays. At Bushmills the process of bottling on the premises provides the final touch in the continuity of control which is exerted from the malted barley to the taste of the whiskey in the glass. The bottling process is a precise operation which requires sustained concentration by the staff who switch roles periodically. To watch the bottling is to be reminded that the production of whiskey today is big business, involving the most complex skills and machinery.

Computer

There is no danger, however, that some day they will make *Old Bushmills* by computer. The manufacture of whiskey has been streamlined by modern technology, but in essence it remains the prerogative of human skills — from the distilling right through to the nosing and blending. Willie MacKay who has spent almost a working lifetime in the business is aware of the advantages of science, but in the world of whiskey it is human beings who still hold the key — just as the evolution of Bushmills whiskeys remains as mysterious as the mellowing of clear liquid inside living wood in the quiet depths of the warehouse. Willie MacKay is a precise man not given to bursts of poetry but he can be poetic about a craft as old as this; "There's magic in it. We are working with nature, with living elements. It is not just manufacturing spirits and mixing whiskeys. We are not mere producers. We are composers. What could be more satisfying or creative than that. . .!"

References

1. "Treasures of the Armada" by Robert Stenuit, translated by Francine Barker. Published by David and Charles, Newton Abbot. pp. 247-248.
2. "The Observer Colour Magazine" October 3, 1982. From "The Loneliness of the Long-Distance Guitar Player" by Tony Palmer page 24.

The styles of the packages and the employees have changed down the years, but "Old Bushmills" itself remains essentially the same.

OLD BUSHMILLS IRISH WHISKEY

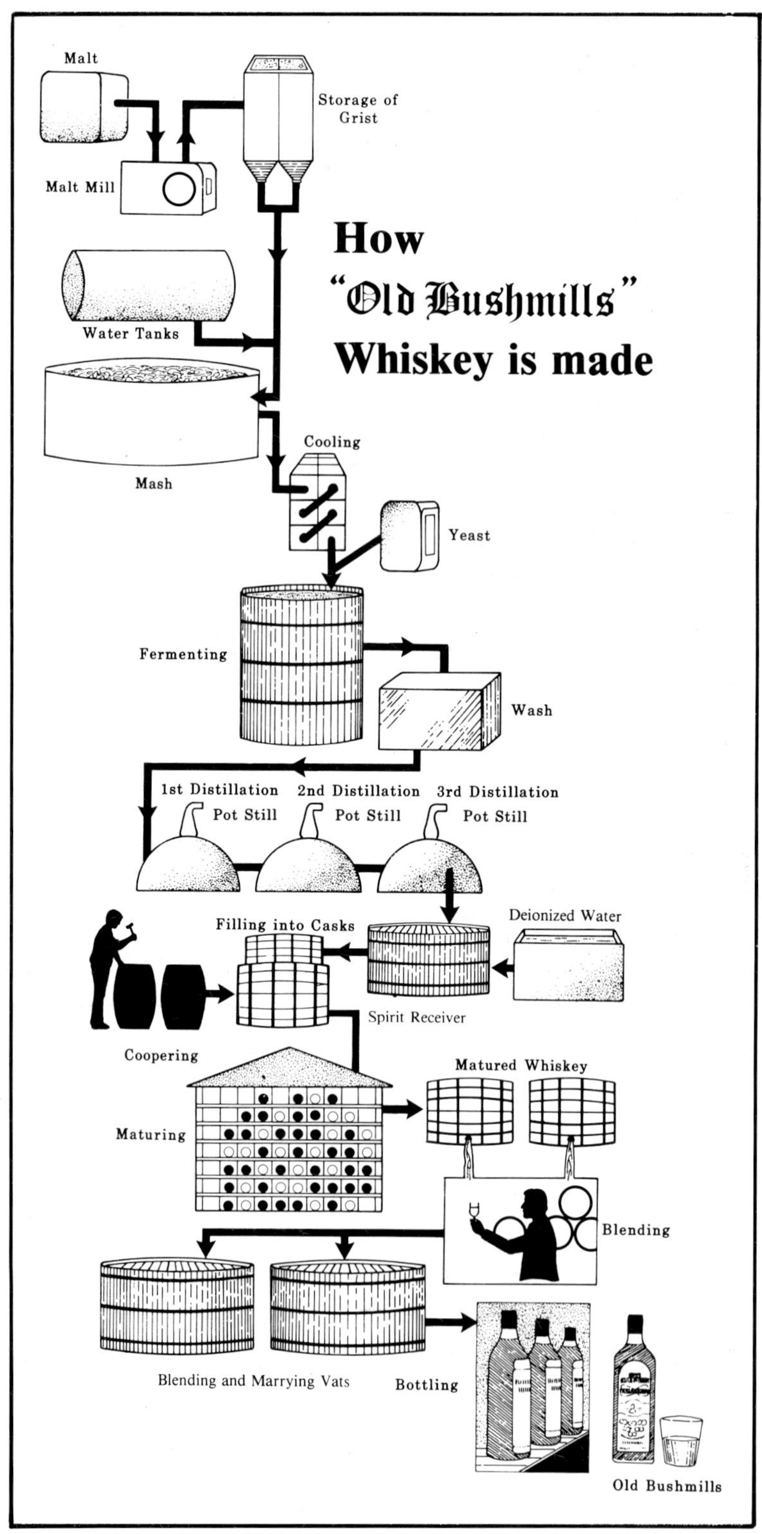

A diagram of the entire production process, including the mashing, fermentation, triple distillation, maturation, blending and finally the bottling.

A display of "Old Bushmills" products in their home and international packaging.

The label for Coleraine Malt from the Distillery that was established in the early 19th Century. It was bought in 1869 by Robert A. Taylor, a member of a well-known Coleraine family.

CHAPTER TEN

Coleraine — "Old Irish"

On Thursday, September 7, 1933, the "Belfast News-Letter", which was founded in 1737 and confidently lays claim to be the oldest surviving daily newspaper in the English-speaking world, carried an important story about *Old Bushmills,* which itself is the world's oldest licensed distillery currently in production.

There were other items of news that morning to inform and to stimulate or perplex the readers. President Roosevelt was taking "extraordinary precautions" for the protection of American citizens in Cuba, following a "coup d'etat" the previous day. In Texas, 32 people were killed and 1,500 injured by a hurricane. In Morocco, the surrender of local tribesmen brought to an end France's 'Little War'. In England the prestigious British Association, at a meeting in Leicester, was turning its attention to the debate "Man versus The Machine," and it counselled the public — prophetically — that "More leisure should not be feared".

However, the story that caught the attention of those with an eye to local business was the news that the *Old Bushmills* Distillery Co. Ltd., had bought over the Coleraine Distillery. Thus began an association which was to last physically for over half-a-century, which was to perpetuate the "Coleraine" brand name that is used even today, and which neatly linked two of the names so closely associated with the *Old Bushmills* story — Sir Thomas Phillips — who was granted the licence "to make Aquavitae etc., in the County of Colrane and the Rowte, Co. Antrim" in 1608, and Wilson Boyd who had just taken over at *Old Bushmills* and was destined to stamp his personality on the company for the next thirty years.

The "Belfast Newsletter" stated; "An announcement yesterday by Messrs. Boyd and Co., of Hill Street, Belfast, of the purchase by them of the Coleraine distillery marks an important development in the whiskey distilling industry in Ulster, and is regarded as a forerunner of other important deals of a similar character in the British Isles.

"Recent events in the United States in regard to the voting on the liquor question have been closely followed by interests in Europe likely to be affected by the result, and no secret has been made of the intention of whiskey distillers and shippers to take full advantage of any change in the American law.

Though Phillips was poorly-regarded by O'Laverty who described him in the 1880's as "unscrupulous and avaricious", he was seen in a rather better perspective by the modern Irish historian Professor T. W. Moody. "When he came to Ireland in the winter of 1598-9, he had seen twenty years' soldiering in the French civil wars. He seems to have been a free-lance and to have served among the English auxiliaries sent by Elizabeth to fight for Henry IV, as well as under Marshal d'Aumont, one of Henry's commanders. He was said to have earned the 'special favour' of the great Henry himself.

"He had also travelled in Spain, Portugal, Italy and Africa, and had learnt to speak French and Spanish. A man in his prime — he must have been about 40 in 1599 — seasoned in warfare, with a wide range of experience and a reputation for courage, energy and trustworthiness, he was given employment in Ireland by Sir Robert Cecil, Elizabeth's principal secretary of state, whose protege he then was and to whom he thereafter acted as a kind of confidential agent. His career abroad had not been a financial success, and he seems to have been pleased enough to seek his fortunes in a new sphere".[2]

"His judgement and valour" soon brought promotion, and during his time at Coleraine in the early years of the 17th century he adapted "part of the old abbey for his own dwelling, and built some small thatched houses for settlers, a water-mill, and fortifications. For the first time a minister of the established church officiated daily, and according to Phillips, the service was well-attended. He also claimed to have spent money freely in developing his market, which not only served the neighbourhood but attracted merchants from Scotland".

Phillips rapidly improved his position — he acquired from the Crown a 21 year lease of the customs at Portrush, Portballintrae and the Bann, and of all ferries over the Bann between Coleraine and Toome at an annual rent of 20s (June, 1605); he was given also a 21 year lease of the castle of Toome, plus 30 acres at a rent of 'one pair of gilded spurs' (18 Feb. 1606); a weekly market and an annual fair at Coleraine, with the usual courts and fees, at a rent of 6s 8d (22 Feb. 1606); in 1607 he received a knighthood; and in 1608 he was granted the licence to make "Aquavitae Etc."

Tenacity

However, King James I and his advisers were unhappy at the response to the opportunities afforded by the Plantation of Ulster. Too few people of the right calibre were applying, and the government, from 1609 onwards, turned for help to the city of London. By "a mixture of persuasion, cajolery and veiled force" the Londoners themselves were induced to develop the area. Phillips had to surrender Coleraine and his other assets and within a few years of the Londoners' advent he engaged them in a controversy which he maintained with great tenacity for a quarter of a century. He claimed that they had failed in work that he could have carried out single-handed. At considerable personal cost, Phillips pursued the matter until in 1635, by which time he was virtually bankrupt, the Court of Star Chamber ruled against the city, imposed a fine of £70,000 and forfeited the lands.

Coleraine developed as an ecclesiastical settlement with an abbey dating from the sixth century, and it was also a centre of great strategic importance. The foundations for the modern town were established here in the 17th century by Sir Thomas Phillips, who was also granted the first licence to distil at Bushmills. This drawing dates from the turn of this century.

Phillips died in August 1636 at his home in Hammersmith "sicke in body, but of sound and perfect memorie". Six children were mentioned in his will, including a son Dudley — the father of the George Phillips who took part in the defence of Derry during the great siege. Among his many bequests, Sir Thomas left his "worst-cloth suit" to his "man" John Deakyn; £10 (and also a new suit and coat) to Thomas, his coachman; £5 to the poor of Fulham; £5, together with a mourning gown, to the preacher of his funeral sermon; and provision for making a Collection of his papers and memoirs — which was never done.

Thus the historical figure whose name is linked so intimately with the official beginnings of *Old Bushmills* emerges from the mists of time not as a shadowy English functionary, but as a man of dedication, tenacity, and a consuming passion to see that justice was done, according to his own standards. He was always anxious to put English interests first, but Professor Moody concludes; "He was a capable man of affairs, who served the English crown faithfully and acted justly according to his lights, in the crude and grasping world of early seventeenth-century Ireland".

Licence

Sir Thomas Phillips is mentioned often enough in the history of that period and in the story of *Old Bushmills,* but one of the earliest references to "Old Coleraine" whiskey is contained in a story from the 12th century version of the Book of Leinster, as related by Canon O'Laverty. He refers to Mesca Ulad, "the intoxication of the Ulstermen", during a feast at Dundabheann near Bushmills. O'Laverty claims that the guests started out for Louth but lost their way "and wandered off to the wilds of Kerry" because they had partaken too freely of "Old Coleraine"![3] This would appear, however, to be no more than a little literary licence.

O'Laverty was using a translation of the story (originally in early 12th century Irish) which was summarised by the Royal Irish Academy in 1880. O'Laverty's own work was published in 1887 when Coleraine malt whiskey was indeed well-established and had a high reputation. It is not unknown for an author to slip a contemporary reference into an ancient story. O'Laverty was straining credibility rather too far in ascribing to "Old Coleraine" a 12th century origin, but the story loses nothing in the telling!

The history of the Coleraine Distillery moves onto much firmer ground in the early part of the 19th century. On July 1, 1837, a Thomas Black advertised in the "Coleraine Chronicle". He stated "The Proprietor is happy to find that his Whiskey has met with such a decided preference; he requests that those who wish to have genuine Malt Whiskey, to be guided by the gentlemen who have already made use of it. A large supply is on sale at his stores, which will be sold cheap for cash or good Bills. Nine gallons is the smallest quantity he can send out".

COLERAINE DISTILLERY.

THE Proprietor is happy to find that his WHISKEY has met with such a decided preference; he requests that those who wish to have genuine MALT WHISKEY, to be guided by the gentlemen who have already made use of it. A large supply on Sale at his Stores, which will be sold cheap for Cash or good Bills. Nine gallons is the smallest quantity he can send out.

THOMAS BLACK.

Coleraine, 1st July, 1837.

The history of Coleraine Distillery moving onto firmer ground.

Old Mill

There are references elsewhere as to the origin of the Coleraine Distillery. According to Alfred Barnard it was "an old manorial mill at the end of the seventeenth century, and was converted into a Distillery in the year 1820''.[4] The writer in ''The Mercantile Age and Textile Times'' in 1888 (a year after the original publication of Barnard) makes the same point — that the mill was converted to a distillery in 1820. Yet another source, dating from *Old Bushmills* itself around 1938, claims that the Coleraine premises were built by John Rennie, a Scotsman, in connection with his business as a flour miller — and that later they were converted into a Distillery.

In the 1840's the Distillery passed into the hands of the Moore family of Moorefort, Ballymoney, who were also owners of the Bann Distillery at Drumaheaglis, a few miles from Ballymoney, and of malting barns at Newmills. An advertisement in the ''Chronicle'' of July 7, 1849 is signed by James Moore who states;

''Owing to the Fine Qualities of this Whiskey the demand for it has so much increased throughout the United Kingdom, that the Proprietor in order to continue its manufacture by that slow process which he has found most valuable in producing a pure spirit; and in order to keep up his stock of Old Whiskey, has doubled the extent of his Malting Establishment. He can supply this Delicious Whiskey ripe and ready for use, Bonded, in Puncheons, Butts, Pipes, Hogsheads, and Quarter Casks, or in any quantity not less than Ten Gallons, from his own stores. Orders, from any part of the United Kingdom, punctually attended to, and Duty Free to foreign countries''.

Moore's reference to the popularity of Coleraine Malt in the United Kingdom is significant because by 1849 it was acquiring its famous advertising slogan ''H.C.''. This was not a reference, as some people still believe today, to its quality when served either ''Hot'' or ''Cold'', but rather to its elevation to the bar in the Westminster House of Commons! It was introduced there in 1845. Some observers have claimed that Coleraine earned its ''H.C.'' label under the ownership of the Taylor family, one of whom was a noted M.P., but the introduction to the House of Commons was made much earlier, possibly by one of the band of Northern Irish Members who sat in the Imperial Parliament.

Taylors

In 1869, the Distillery was bought by Robert A. Taylor, a member of a well-known Coleraine family. He was chairman of Coleraine Town Commissioners, a member of the Londonderry Grand Jury, a representative of the Coleraine Division of Londonderry County Council, and a vice-president of the Board of Governors of Coleraine Academical Institution. He was knighted in 1899. His brother Daniel was equally, if not more, distinguished. He was Liberal MP for Coleraine in the Westminster Parliament from 1874-1880, chairman of the Coleraine Town Commissioners in 1864, 1865 and 1873, and High Sheriff of the City and County of Londonderry in 1885.

According to a private history in the possession of the family (which is thought to have been written by Daniel Taylor) their father was born at Carnabuoy, near Bushmills in May, 1785. His own father, John, had been a blacksmith. Daniel

Taylor senior worked in England, Scotland and in Belfast and in 1815 started a grocery business in Coleraine.[5]

He died in 1845, but a personal portrait by his son Daniel gives something of the flavour of the man. "In the month of August, 1815 he commenced the grocery business in Coleraine. He was then in the zenith of his life. Thirty years before this he was born. Thirty years after it he died . . . He was in business seven years when he married, and during this time he wrought very hard and being the greater part of this time alone he was unable to get his food regularly, yet he enjoyed even this season of slaving, having a few kind friends and neighbours with whom he spent many pleasant evenings.

"He was very fond of the prose versions of David's Psalms and I have often seen him even in Church when the Minister was preaching in a strain he cared not for hearing—I may just here mention he disliked controversial sermons and particularly those directed against Roman Catholics in which he thought (with all respect to the Presbyterian preachers) they from the heat of passion in which many of them enter into this subject made statements against this class of characters that were ungrounded — under such a sermon as this he would turn over some of David's Psalms and read those with particularly pleasure in which there was no discordance."

By 1861 the family firm of D. and R. Taylor were well-established grocers and seed merchants, and when Robert Taylor entered into the distilling trade eight years later he lost no time in capitalising on the good name of his family and of Coleraine Whiskey. In May, 1869 he announced, "Having purchased the Coleraine Distillery from the representatives of the late Mr. James Moore, I have now commenced distilling. The whole premises are in the most perfect order. The very finest pure Malt Spirit will be produced and every care given to maintain the previous high character of the Distillery. I have also bought all the old Coleraine Whiskey reserved at the Auction and bonded at Coleraine, Belfast and Ballymena. I am, therefore, in a position to offer both Old and New Whiskey. Hoping to be favoured with your orders, which will have my prompt attention."

Civil War

Under the proprietorship of Robert Taylor, the whiskey enhanced its reputation and references to "Coleraine malt" cropped up in the most unexpected places. It is mentioned by James Dunwody Bulloch in his book "The Secret Service of the Confederate States in Europe". At the outbreak of the American Civil War, the Confederate Government had few naval resources and had to equip its forces urgently from abroad. Bulloch was selected as a Confederate secret agent in Europe. His job was to oversee the construction and despatch of suitable vessels, and the two-volume report of his work is regarded as a Civil War classic.

He describes how the Alabama left Liverpool (under an assumed name) and anchored off the Irish coast before continuing her journey. Subsequently she captured, sank or burned 68 ships in 22 months before being sunk herself in 1864. She drove Union ships off the high seas for virtually two years and caused more than

The Alabama, the Confederate vessel which virtually drove Union ships off the high seas for two years during the American Civil War. On her maiden voyage from England she anchored off the North of Ireland — hence her connection with the Causeway Coast and "the best of Coleraine malt".

6 million US dollars damage and the claims arising from her actions led to a test case which became significant in international law.

Bulloch gives a detailed description of her movements along the Irish Coast as she ventured out from her supposed anonymity in England, for the first time.

"(We) entered between Rathlin Island and Fair Head . . . stopped the engines off the Giant's Causeway, hailed a fishing-boat, and Bond and I went ashore in a pelting rain, leaving Captain Butcher to proceed with the Enrica in accordance with his instructions.

"During the evening it rained incessantly, and the wind skirled and snifted about the gables of the hotel in fitful squalls. Bond and I sat comfortably enough in the snug dining-room after dinner, and sipped our toddy, of the best Coleraine malt; but my heart was with the little ship buffeting her way around that rugged north coast of Ireland. I felt sure that Butcher would keep his weather-eye open, and once clear of Innistrahull, there would be plenty of sea-room; but I could not shake off an occasional sense of uneasiness.

"The next morning, August Ist, Bond and I took a boat and pulled along the coast to Port Rush. The weather was beautifully fine, and the effect of the bright sun and the gentle west wind was so exhilarating that I felt no further solicitude about the Enrica. (This was the code name for the Alabama.) From Port Rush we took rail to Belfast, and then steamer and rail, via Fleetwood to Liverpool."[6]

That was in 1862. Twelve years later, Coleraine Malt was still making news, this time in the Coleraine Chronicle.

"Amongst the presents from Ireland to H.R.H. the Duke of Edinburgh, on the occasion of his marriage with the Princess Marie Alexandrowna of Russia, was a somewhat unique one, ordered to be forwarded, direct from the Coleraine Distillery, by Alexander Watson, Esq., M.D., R.N. It consists of a cask of the very finest Coleraine Whiskey, and was despatched to Buckingham Palace on Tuesday last. The cask, which is made of fine oak, French polished, and clasped with burnished copper hoops, bears on one end the Coleraine arms, and on the other a solid silver shield — surrounded by the name of the proprietor of the distillery, R. A. Taylor Esq., — on which is engraved the following; 'From Dr. A. Watson, R.N., to His Royal Highness the Duke of Edinburgh, January 1874."

"It will be recollected that it was Dr. Watson who extracted the ball from His Royal Highness' person, which was fired at him by an assassin in Melbourne some years ago, and who afterwards became his private medical adviser on board the Galatea. The quality of the liquor in the Duke's cask cannot be surpassed for mellowness, purity and delicious aroma, and has been already designated by all who have had the good fortune of tasting it, "The Royal Blend." Dr. Watson, who has for years enjoyed the personal friendship of 'England's sailor prince' will, we are sure, receive His Royal Highness' cordial thanks for bringing under his notice the 'nectar of the gods' and the very panacea for 'all the ills to which flesh is heir.' "

No. of Message..................

POST OFFICE TELEGRAPHS.

Dated Stamp of ... Office.

Harrison & Sons, London.

If the accuracy of an Inland Telegram be doubted, the telegram will be repeated on payment of half the amount originally paid for its transmission, any fraction of 1d. less than ½d. being reckoned as ½d.; and if it be found that there was any inaccuracy, the amount paid for repetition will be refunded. Special conditions are applicable to the repetition of Foreign Telegrams.

N.B.—This Form must accompany any inquiry made respecting this Telegram.

Charges to pay £..........s..........d.

Handed in at the Coleraine Office at 4.12 P.M., Received here at ....M.

TO Robt A Taylor Queens Hotel Manch

Unanimously appointed Chrman Town Commissrs on motion of Nelin Second by Henry Nevin Colerai

A telegram in 1887 informing Robert Taylor that he had been appointed Chairman of the Coleraine Town Commissioners.

Coleraine Temperance Cafe

This café is one of the finest and best equipped in Ireland

It is centrally situated in Queen Street, within a minute's walk from the Town Hall. Its principal Dining Room accommodates almost 100 at a time. Tariff very moderate. Tourists and Summer Visitors at Portrush or Portstewart paying a visit to Coleraine will find the Café the most convenient place for Refreshments. Commercial gentlemen are specially catered for.

The Café includes a large room suitable for Receptions, Concerts, etc., also a Ladies' Private Room, etc.

MISS ANNA S. GRAY, *Manageress*

In 1892 a Temperance Cafe was opened in Coleraine. The accommodation included stabling "for at least one hundred and fifty horses . . ." This was because a Temperance establishment had to offer equally good or better stabling than that provided by local public houses. The site of the restaurant was later occupied by a restaurant.

Temperance

The Taylor family was making headlines in other ways too. When Daniel Taylor stood for Parliament in 1874 he wrote a letter to the voters and presented his views on the leading questions of the day. Despite the pre-occupation of his younger brother with distilling, he was firm about Temperance; "I shall support such a measure for the Closing of Public Houses on Sundays as that indicated in Sir Dominic Corrigan's Bill; and any other well-conceived and carefully digested plan for mitigating the growing evils of Intemperance shall receive my most earnest consideration."

(In 1892 a Temperance Cafe was opened in Coleraine. According to the Coleraine Chronicle "Such an establishment is much-needed in Coleraine, and the warmest thanks of the community are due to the public-spirited lady who in her lifetime confers a boon upon the town in which she has manifested such a practical interest." The report outlines in detail the accommodation provided not only for customers, but also for horses. Any Temperance establishment needed to equal and indeed to improve upon the stabling offered by local public houses. So in the new Temperance Restaurant there was "accommodation for at least a hundred and fifty horses. . . . There are also ample spaces for carts, and every accommodation here for the servants of farmers." Farm labourers and their families went in the back door, and farmers and their families generally entered by the front!)

Praise

While the Coleraine Distillery was furthering its reputation at home and abroad — it was said that 'old Coleraine' was so smooth that even a teetotaller would not have known he was drinking whiskey — there was an enthusiastic reception from the trade Press, and from distinguished visitors like Alfred Barnard. He noted; "Here we must pause to say that, in all our wanderings through Erin's Green Isle, for cleanliness, order and regularity, we have seen no Distillery to beat this. The Stillmen seem to take a delight and pride in their work, and regard all these old Pot Stills with veneration. They are kept as shining as gold, and every bit of brass work, even the frames of the Safe and Sampling Safe, were polished and bright enough for a jeweller's show case."[7]

A year later, in 1888, the writer in the "Mercantile Age and Textile Times" was equally fulsome in his praise. "At home and abroad I have visited about seventeen hundred industrial establishments, including a great number of distilleries and breweries, and as a class they are the cleanest establishments I have visited, but never in the whole course of my existence have I visited a distillery that has been so scrupulously clean, and in saying this I am but reuttering the opinion of Mr. Alfred Barnard, who has visited more distilleries than any other writer. Mr. Edward Reid, the firm's distiller, certainly takes a great pride in keeping up his utensils, which are principally of beautiful wrought-copper, the ceilings, walls, and floors of his various houses and rooms, in a spotless condition."

The writer added "Though (Coleraine whiskey) has been freely exhibited to all the world and his wife at the Manchester, Edinburgh, Glasgow and the Irish Exhibition at Olympia, it has only once been put in a competition, and that was the Edinburgh Exhibition 1886, where it received from the jurors the Highest Pure Malt Distillers' Award."

If that was not praise enough, a writer in the Constitution in May 1892 was ecstatic about his visit, and his sampling of a Coleraine Malt of 1851. "Here in this catacomb lives and thrives Coleraine malt, 41 years old spirit of the ages. A dead silence prevails, whilst the heart alone beats to the praise and glory of old Coleraine malt, vintage 1851. Words are fools to describe the sample; water would insult it; it rolls down with a smoothness and a cleanness leaving a flavour on the tongue of beautiful Coleraine, yet withal bearing an unmistakable similarity to the Coleraine of today."

Coleraine whiskey owed its excellence to the craftsmen who made it, but as with *Old Bushmills* the supply of water was vital — and special in an ecclesiastical way. It is said that the Coleraine well was blessed by St. Finian of Movilla in the 6th century, while on a visit to Carbreus, Bishop of Coleraine!

Demise

Despite the Taylors' commercial success, the passage of time had cast its shadow across the family. In 1889 Daniel Taylor, the former MP, died. In a fulsome obituary, the Coleraine Chronicle stated; "Success in life did not turn his head as the manner of too many is. If he knew you thirty years ago or more, he knew you to the last."

Robert Taylor outlived his brother by 13 years, but he gradually slipped into failing health. In 1884 his friends entertained him to a picnic on the banks of the River Bush. The purpose, according to the indefatigable Coleraine Chronicle, was "to congratulate him on his recovery from his late severe accident, and on his return to renewed health and strength from a trip to the Mediterreanean and the continent, whither he had gone by advice of his medical adviser."

However he had recovered sufficiently to travel to America in 1893, and the Coleraine Commissioners held a Complimentary Dinner in his honour at the Clothworkers' Arms Hotel on June 27th. The guests enjoyed an extensive menu which included turtle soup, salmon, sole, sweetbreads, mutton, roast beef, roast lamb, boiled chicken, ham, duckling, mayonnaise of lobster, red currant and raspberry tarts, gooseberry tarts, wine and liqueur jellies, ice pudding a la Nesselrode, and fresh fruit. Refreshments included milk punch, hock, sherry, champagne, liqueurs and claret. The Victorians knew how to celebrate!

There was also more than a little humour about Coleraine. One famous story concerning Sir Robert Taylor involved a "Stamper" Thompson, who sported a wooden leg and a ready line in "poetry", like a Victorian Secundus MacGonagall. The worthy "Stamper" was brought before the magistrates, including Sir Robert, on a charge of being drunk and incapable which, with a wooden leg, sounds not

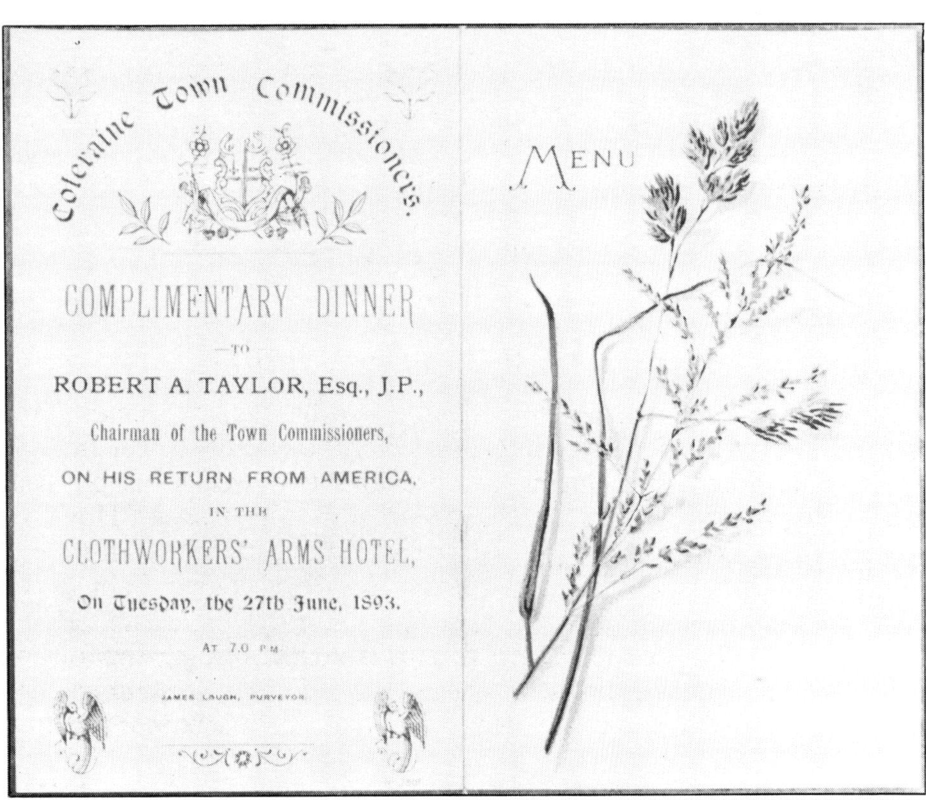

Coleraine Town Commissioners.

COMPLIMENTARY DINNER

—TO—

ROBERT A. TAYLOR, Esq., J.P.,

Chairman of the Town Commissioners,

ON HIS RETURN FROM AMERICA,

IN THE

CLOTHWORKERS' ARMS HOTEL,

On Tuesday, the 27th June, 1893.

AT 7.0 P.M.

JAMES LAUGH, PURVEYOR.

MENU

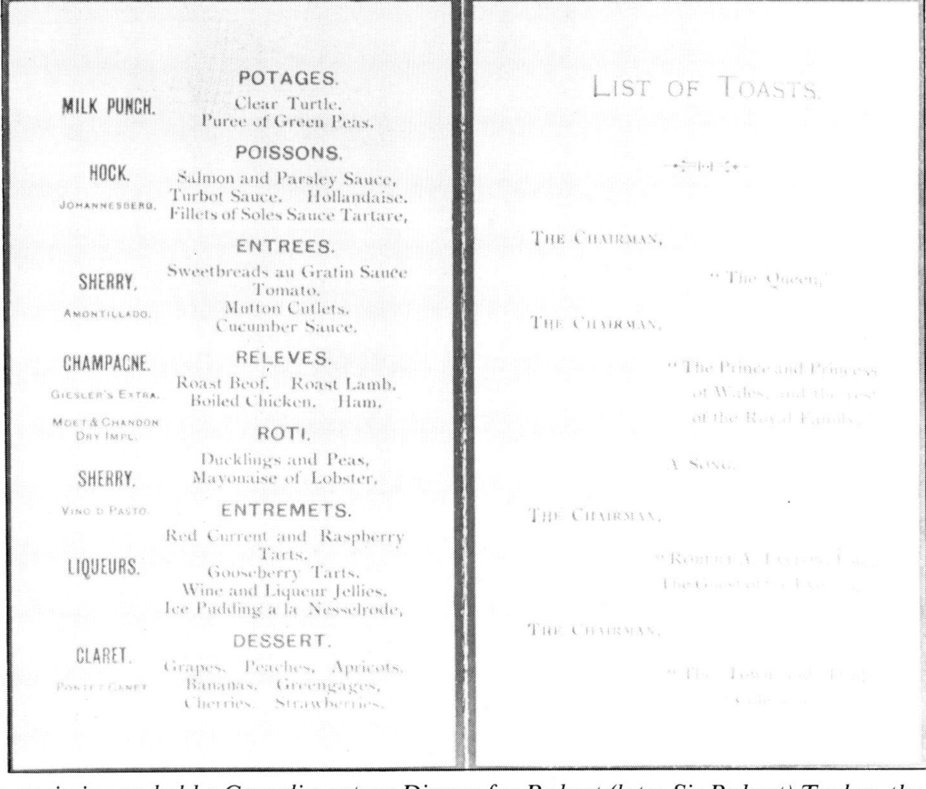

MILK PUNCH.

HOCK.
JOHANNESBERG.

SHERRY.
AMONTILLADO.

CHAMPAGNE.
GIESLER'S EXTRA.
MOET & CHANDON DRY IMPL.

SHERRY.
VINO D PASTO.

LIQUEURS.

CLARET.
PONTET CANET

POTAGES.
Clear Turtle.
Puree of Green Peas.

POISSONS.
Salmon and Parsley Sauce,
Turbot Sauce. Hollandaise.
Fillets of Soles Sauce Tartare,

ENTREES.
Sweetbreads au Gratin Sauce Tomato.
Mutton Cutlets.
Cucumber Sauce.

RELEVES.
Roast Beef. Roast Lamb.
Boiled Chicken. Ham.

ROTI.
Ducklings and Peas,
Mayonaise of Lobster.

ENTREMETS.
Red Current and Raspberry Tarts.
Gooseberry Tarts.
Wine and Liqueur Jellies.
Ice Pudding a la Nesselrode,

DESSERT.
Grapes. Peaches. Apricots.
Bananas. Greengages.
Cherries. Strawberries.

LIST OF TOASTS.

THE CHAIRMAN,
"The Queen."

THE CHAIRMAN,
"The Prince and Princess of Wales, and the rest of the Royal Family."

A SONG.

THE CHAIRMAN,
"ROBERT A. TAYLOR, [illegible]"

THE CHAIRMAN,
"The Town and [illegible]"

The Coleraine Commissioners held a Complimentary Dinner for Robert (later Sir Robert) Taylor, the proprietor of the local Distillery, and a much-respected public figure. The guests enjoyed an extensive menu, in grand Victorian style.

unreasonable. Sir Robert was sharing the bench with Vance Macauley, a local farmer. When asked how he pleaded "Stamper" replied;

> "Vance Macauley grew the barley,
> Robert Taylor brewed the Malt,
> 'Stamper' Thompson drank the whiskey
> So who the deil's at fault?"

Nobleman

Robert Taylor continued to prosper commercially, and his greatest honour was that of a knighthood in 1899. Three years later, however, he was dead. On June 14 the Coleraine Chronicle noted that during the previous two weeks his physical condition had been causing anxiety, but that there was some improvement. However on June 17 it reported that Sir Robert Taylor JP, aged 72, had passed "from time to eternity." And in an obituary as fulsome as that for his brother Daniel, the newspaper stated; ". . . Sir Robert's intimate friends recognise with intense sadness that the end of a notable life has been reached. It is in the spirit of mourning for one of nature's noblemen that we lay a wreath upon his tomb and write as an epitaph that he was 'full of mercy and good works, without partiality and without hypocrisy'."

The death of Daniel Taylor in 1889, and that of his brother Sir Robert thirteen years later, brought to an end a distinctive chapter in the story of the Coleraine Distillery.

DEATH OF

SIR ROBERT A. TAYLOR, J.P.,

COLERAINE.

In the death of Sir Robert A. Taylor, J.P., Coleraine has lost one who was in a very special sense a useful citizen, and who for a great many years was closely identified with, and anxious for, its progress and prosperity. It would be hard to mention any local movement during the last thirty or forty years in which he did not take a leading part; indeed, so numerous were the public duties entrusted to him, and so conscientiously were they fulfilled, that when a few years ago his health began to fail, and he was unable to devote the same attention to them, there was scarcely an institution in the town that did not feel the loss of his assistance to a greater or less extent; and latterly, when he was laid aside altogether, his absence and its cause were much deplored. At different times his wonderful vitality was manifested in a renewal of strength sufficient to enable him to pay cherished visits to many friends in the neighbourhood, but these intervals, unfortunately, were of brief duration, and time after time the hopes entertained of permanent recovery were disappointed. Towards the close of last week the indications pointed only too plainly to the approach of death, and although on Monday

THE LATE DANIEL TAYLOR, Esq., J.P.

PULPIT REFERENCES.

NEW-ROW PRESBYTERIAN CHURCH.

On Sabbath last, in New-row Presbyterian Church, Coleraine, Rev. R. Wallace preached an able sermon from St. John's Gospel, eleventh chapter, and 32nd verse—"Lord, if thou hadst been here, my brother had not died." The entire service was appropriate to the solemn occasion, and the congregation seemed to feel deeply the loss of their most esteemed fellow-worshipper. At the close of the sermon Rev. Mr. Wallace said—This subject, brethren, very naturally and properly suggests to us the recent loss sustained by us, by the whole surrounding community, and especially by the bereaved family, through the removal by death of Mr. Daniel Taylor, who was brought up in connection with this congregation, and for many years was an exemplary, useful, and generous member of its managing committee. For some time past friends were grieved whilst observing the visible decline which appeared and seemed to continue in Mr. Taylor's health. The slower gait, the absence of the characteristic cheerfulness and buoyancy, and his partial retirement from the customary employments of an active life, all furnishing painful evidence that the keepers of the house were beginning to tremble, and the strong men to bow themselves. During a somewhat lengthened illness he bore without murmur the varied and wasting afflictions sent upon him. When he learned that there was no hope of recovery he bowed submissively to what he re- ... as the will of God, and in the exercise of ... and hope awaited the end.

Bann Bridge, Coleraine.

These picture postcard studies of Coleraine date from the turn of this century. The town with its neat lines is one of the more attractive settlements in the North of Ireland.

Church Street. Coleraine.

Thus ended a significant chapter in the story of the Coleraine Distillery. Robert Taylor was succeeded by his nephew Andrew Clarke and the story of Coleraine Distillery moved through the war years to its acquisition by another noted family, the Boyds. They bought not only the stocks and buildings but they also inherited the high reputation of a whiskey that had been carefully nurtured for 64 years by the Taylor family and their successors.

Renewal

The plant was not in operation when the Boyds took over. According to a document published by the Company, the manufacture of whiskey at the Coleraine Distillery was discontinued about 1924 but restarted in the late Thirties. An information sheet published in 1938 stated; "The enhanced prospects in Coleraine's oldest industry are due chiefly to the efforts of the young and energetic local manager Mr. J. W. Morrison, who with conspicuous ability, planned and carried out the renovations and modernisation of the building and plant . . . Six months intensive reconstruction work at the Distillery culminate at the beginning of this week in the recommencement of the process of distillation. It takes a week to evolve the spirit which requires years to reach mature perfection. At the present moment whiskey is running from the stills which have been unemployed for a decade and a half, and is well up to the standard of former years. But it will be a long time before it is ready for sale as the mellowed, finished product."

Jimmy Morrison was manager not only of Coleraine but also of *Old Bushmills* and of the old Killowen Distillery which the Boyds had bought to use for the malting of barley. Morrison, a farmer's son, learned the distilling business in Scotland. He worked in the *Old Bushmills* complex from 1931 to 1955 and earned the reputation of being strict, but fair. One employee recalls; "I can still see him standing there at 5.30 am checking the workers in. There were no time-clocks in those days. He was a hard man. If you were found taking drink on the job, he was very tough. There were no second-chances. But he was also straight and fair, and he had a sense of humour. We called him 'Cracker-Heels!' because he used to wear steel tips on the heels of his shoes!"

Memoirs

Jimmy Morrison, in his memoirs "Over 50 years in Distilleries" (which were written for his family) confirms his peppery character, his directness and his sense of humour. "I will admit that I do not have a slow temper, and many former workers under me will testify to this. But I hope that everyone will admit that after a telling-off it was immediately forgotten. In fact many waited until I took off my hat and clouted them over the side of the head! They knew the incident was forgiven and forgotten for good."

Morrison was a self-made man who undertook a five-year training course with the Mortlach Distillery at Dufftown. He was paid £2-18-0 a week with "no set hours, day or night." He spent three years on practical work and then he did a two-year course at Birmingham University in one, much to the delight and surprise of his employers, who promptly refunded the £300 for the second-year which he had paid himself. Then after several more years he came to *Old Bushmills*.

When he took over, he had to do a great deal of work to improve the operating capacity of the plant. He helped to persuade the Boyds to invest in more and better equipment, and his staff increased in his first year from four to eleven. He recalls, with typical directness "On my arrival I had a staff of four. Ben Johnston was a stillman and handyman and a really reliable employee, even if he did give me a telling off one July 12th for painting my dog green!"

Gradually the *Old Bushmills* operation was streamlined and expanded, and he had to turn his attention to the Killowen Distillery which needed renovation to make it suitable for malting barley. "Killowen" he writes "was a real shambles," but with determination and hard work it eventually provided valuable space for malting.

Decision to Buy

The Boyds' decision to buy the Coleraine Distillery created further challenges and Jimmy Morrison and the staff had to turn their attention to making yet another plant operative. With the war looming, the Coleraine project "was temporarily shelved". Barley was rationed, and a number of employees joined the Armed Services.

Despite the Second World War there were lighter moments. "We obtained in 1939 an ex-Belfast fire engine, chain driven and complete with solid rubber tyres. . . In the village of Bushmills the stationer's shop went on fire. The building was well alight before the fire unit got there, but it made short work of dousing the flames. The hand signal to stop pumping was mistaken by the driver. He thought more water was needed so he opened the throttle. As a result the whole front wall was pushed down, and the shops and houses on the opposite side of the street had a free wash!"

After the war, however, the Coleraine Distillery came into its own. The Luftwaffe air raid on Belfast in 1941 had damaged not only the *Old Bushmills* head offices and stores but also the bottling plant. Therefore the bottling was transferred to Coleraine, and stayed there until the Sixties when it was established at Bushmills itself. In the meantime, Coleraine continued to produce its malt whiskey, but in the mid-Fifties the Boyds decided to manufacture their own grain whiskey. So Coleraine began to produce grain for blending with Bushmills malt, as well as grain for its own brand of Coleraine whiskey. However the last run of Coleraine malt, known as "Coleraine HC," was produced in the early Sixties and it is thought that only a half-dozen casks exist today.

Coleraine Town Hall is a focal point, and it is featured even today on the packaging for Coleraine Whiskey. The front view, with bunting and Victory Arch shows part of the celebrations at the end of the First World War. The back view is a picture by William Alfred Green and dates from the early 1900's. Note the monument at the back of the Town Hall. This is a memorial to Andrew Orr, JP, a local linen bleacher, and his family.

Grain Whiskey

Still in the mid-Fifties, however, Jimmy Morrison was faced with another challenge — to start a grain-distilling operation in a plant that was used to making potstill malt whiskey. He recalls "I told the Boyds that grain plant and production was not my line" but he had to get on with the job.

Grain whiskey is so-called because unmalted cereals like maize and rye are used as well as malted barley. The liquid drawn off the mixture of cereals, which are mashed together, is fermented as in the production of malt whiskey. Distillation takes place in a "Coffey" or "patent" still. Re-charging does not take place as in a potstill, which requires three separate distillations to produce the liquid that will become Irish whiskey. In the Coffey still, production is continuous and the end -product is a spirit which is used for blending. The invention of this type of still by Aeneas Coffey, a Dubliner who became Inspector General of Excise in Ireland and later a distiller, revolutionised the spirit industry. He offered his invention to distillers in Ireland but the vast majority spurned the offer and argued that the best whiskey was the variety produced from the potstill.

Unhappily for the Irish, the Scottish distillers soon discovered the advantages of using grain with malt, and they laid the foundation of the Scottish blended whisky industry which later vastly outsold Irish whiskey. Subsequently, the Irish came to appreciate fully the value of the "Coffey" or "patent" still and the industry has made considerable progress, particularly in recent years.

Having launched the grain spirit process at Coleraine, Jimmy Morrison faced yet more challenges, and not the least of these was to keep an eye on "Mary Craig's" public house. "By this time I had quite a full day with *Old Bushmills* Distillery and Maltings, Killowen Maltings, Coleraine Malt Distillery, Coleraine Grain Distillers, the bottling plant at Coleraine and all the odd jobs that bottling entails. Then the boss had to 'overload the donkey' by buying 'Mary Craigs.' Looking after a pub was a full time job, and in fact it was easier doing all my other work!"

Farewell

Around this period, however, Morrison received an offer from Chivas Regal which he literally could not afford to refuse. So he went to Scotland on a higher salary and to a better house. But significantly, he noted; "The evening I accepted the job I posted my resignation to Belfast and asked to be released as soon as possible. This was refused and I was told that I would have to work three months notice. From then on Mr Wilson Boyd neither visited the Distilleries, nor phoned nor wrote to me."

So James Watt Morrison and his wife Maisie left Ireland after 24 years. Later he expressed regrets, despite the attractions of the new job. "We really loved being in Northern Ireland. Of course there were ups and downs, but we made many friends. The people of the Coleraine — Bushmills area are the salt of the earth!"

The Distilleries, despite those "ups and downs" had their characters, and none more so than those at Coleraine. John MacLennan, who joined in the Mid-Fifties,

Jimmy Morrison, who spent 24 years as the manager at "Old Bushmills". A Scot with a peppery character, a direct approach and a sense of humour, he was respected for his discipline, and fairness. He retired to Scotland but looked back on Ulster with great affection; "The people of the Coleraine-Bushmills area are the salt of the earth."

recalls; "The place was old, even archaic but people worked really hard. There was a great sense of atmosphere, and many of the people were larger than life. Stewart Whitley, the Chief Clerk, had an agricultural turn of phrase, and John Clark, the Customs and Excise officer, was equally expressive. I remember him taking me aside and saying 'Now that you have joined the business, let me give you a word of advice. Whiskey makes a good walking stick for the journey through life, but it's a damn bad crutch!"

Phasing Out

Though the last of the Coleraine malt was made in the mid-Sixties the Distillery continued to produce grain for blending with Bushmills malt and for the production of the "Coleraine Whiskey" brand. But from 1978 the Distillery began to be phased out. The decision was partly economic and partly environmental. By this time *Old Bushmills* had become part of the Irish Distillers Group which had facilities for making extensive quantities of grain whiskey at their Midleton Distillery in Cork. Secondly, any expansion of the Coleraine Distillery to meet the increased demand would have not only been costly but extremely difficult physically. The Distillery was in the middle of a town with limited scope for physical expansion, and increased production would have required a compliance with strict health regulations in terms of effluent and environmental control. Even with the best will in the world, this would have been difficult. Given all these factors the decision was taken, albeit sadly, to phase out the Coleraine Distillery.

There are still sufficient supplies of the old Coleraine grain for the production of Bushmills whiskeys as well as the current "Coleraine" brand, but in time the grain supplied from Midleton will be introduced. Already Midleton grain has been transported to Bushmills to mature. Despite all the changes, and the passage of time, the name lives on today in the "Coleraine Irish Whiskey" brand, with its distinctive label and the picture of the Town Hall, so redolent of the long history of Old Coleraine.

Affection

From the early 19th century, Coleraine whiskey had had an honoured name, a high reputation, and a place in the affection and the folk-lore of the people of the area, as well as much further afield. The character and affection are well summarised in the song written by James Feehan, a Tipperary man who at one time was a teacher in Coleraine Model School. Apparently James Feehan organised two concerts each year — one by the pupils and one by his friends. On the morning of one of these concerts he wrote the words of the song himself whilst in class between 10.00 and 12.30 am:

"The Spaniard may boast of his sherry
The Frenchman his sparkling champagne,
But if a man wants to be merry,
I'd advise him to try 'Old Coleraine'.

You may search in the annals of history
To the time of the Roman and Dane
But you'll find it was reckoned a mystery,
How they made such good stuff in Coleraine.

Chorus
"Then hurrah! for the 'trim little Borough'
And the Bann as it flows through the plain;
Its waters will banish all sorrow
When mixed with a drop of 'Coleraine.'

Cleopatra once gave a great banquet,
And sent for her wines off to Spain,
But, knowing Mark Antony's 'wakeness',
She got in a cask of Coleraine.
And old Bacchus himself when a-boozing
Found that wine next day gave his head pain,
So he quit it, and then took to using
A drop o the rale 'Oul Coleraine'

This potstill was formerly used in the Coleraine Distillery and is now the centre-piece of the Potstill Bar at "Old Bushmills". It was built by Blair, Campbell and McLean of Glasgow and dates from 1875. The cask of whiskey (bottom right) is one of the last of the Coleraine Malt, dating from 1962. It is thought that only half a dozen casks were left by the early 1980's. The story and taste of "Coleraine HC" had a flavour all its own.

A study of the Coleraine Distillery (top) and an early picture of the Old Killowen Distillery. Both are now closed.

You have all heard of Barney McCleary
And the buttermilk watering the plain
And the pitcher, the pride of the dairy,
That Kitty got smashed near Coleraine.
Now I'll tell you a secret this minute
I'm sure you'll not tell it again,
Of milk not a taste there was in it;
She was smuggling a drop o' Coleraine."

"Our great legislators well know it,
Tis' not in St. James'es in vain;
By thundering speeches-they show it
Inspiration all comes from Coleraine.
If inclined to be thin don't refuse it
Of spareness you won't long complain
At the Guildhall the Aldermen use it
And get all their fat from Coleraine!"

References

1. "An Historical Account of the Diocese of Down and Connor, Ancient and Modern" by the Reverend James O'Laverty, M.R.I.A., Fellow of the Royal Historical and Archaeological Association of Ireland. Parish Priest of Holywood. Vol. IV. Published in 1887 by James Duffy and Sons, 15, Wellington Quay, Dublin, and 1a Paternoster Row, London. pp. 160-162.
2. "Sir Thomas Phillips of Limavady, Servitor" by T. W. Moody. Irish Historical Studies — the joint journal of the Irish Historical Society and the Ulster Society for Irish Historical Studies. Joint editors R. Dudley Edwards and T. W. Moody. Vol. I 1938-39. Dublin Hodges, Figgis and Co. Oxford R. H. Blackwell Ltd. pp. 251-272. (I am indebted to Professor Moody for this detailed study of Phillips which sheds valuable light on a character who is central to the early story of *Old Bushmills).*
3. O'Laverty. Op. Cit. pp. 159-160.
4. "The Whisky Distilleries of the United Kingdom" by Alfred Barnard, published first in 1887 by Harper's Weekly Gazette, and republished in 1969 by David and Charles Reprints, Newton Abbot Devon, Page 435.
5. A short account of the Taylors and other Coleraine families is contained in "Coleraine in Modern Times" by the Reverend T. H. Mullin D.D., printed in Belfast by Century Services Ltd. 1979. pp. 132-146.
6. "The Secret Service of the Confederate States in Europe or How the Confederate Cruisers Were Equipped" by James D. Bulloch Vol. I and II, with a new introduction by Philip Van Doren Stern. Published by Thomas Yoseloff, New York and London 1959. pp. 242-243.
7. Alfred Barnard Op. Cit. Page 436.

Invitation to
The
375th Anniversary Celebration
of the granting of
The Licence to distil for
The
"Old Bushmills" Distillery

"Old Bushmills" Garden Party

"OLD BUSHMILLS"

THE "OLD BUSHMILLS" DISTILLERY CO. LTD. 1608

To mark the
375th Anniversary
1608 - 1983
Tuesday 21st June 1983

The 375th Anniversary was celebrated by a garden-party at the Distillery. Friends of "Old Bushmills" from far and wide shared the glorious sunshine of mid-summer day and the sense of history on a memorable occasion.

CHAPTER ELEVEN

"Old Bushmills" People

The inherent difficulty about generalising was well-summarised by Alexandre Dumas — "Dumas Fils" — the 19th century French playright and novelist. He stated "All generalisations are dangerous, even this one!" Nevertheless, at the risk of oversimplification it might be said that there are two main kinds of *Old Bushmills* people — the men and women and the families of those who work and have worked in the Distillery, and the many thousands who visit *Old Bushmills* or acquire its taste and who come from all parts of the world.

There is yet another smaller band of *Old Bushmills* people who link together the past and present, tradition and innovation, the visitor and the resident. Typical of these is Jimmy Kane, the Chief Tour Guide and hitherto the "general factotum" who was born virtually within the shadow of the Distillery and has spent a lifetime absorbing and studying its character and its ways. It is not so much that Jimmy supervises a tour — rather he holds together an audience and sizes up each one with the sure touch of a professional entertainer who knows the importance of timing and the chemistry of humanity.

In each group, he believes, there are three basic types — tourists, drinkers and those who are keenly interested in the production process. Jimmy can spot each type fairly quickly, and he reacts accordingly. By the time the group has left the Tun Room, the first stop on their tour, the level of rapport is established. Jimmy says "Over the years you learn how to approach an audience. The tourists move through fairly quickly, but the people with the searching questions tend to stay in the memory. I've heard American visitors say in the Still-Room, "Gee, this reminds me of the smell back home when they're making 'Moonshine!' "

Occasionally there are probing questions from those nearer home. "I notice when they ask details about the size of the still and the production process. I don't say anything direct, but I know that they are likely to be the kind of boys who would make poteen!"

Hospitality

When the tour of the Distillery has been completed the visitors move to the Potstill Bar, where Jimmy Kane dispenses liquid refreshment and some uncommon common sense in roughly equal proportions. "You have to ensure that people enjoy

Some of the plaques presented to ''Old Bushmills'' are displayed in the Potstill Bar and are a tangible reminder of the visitors from all over the world.

themselves, without actually overdoing it, and to steer the conversation accordingly. Sometimes you get special moments that are ingrained in your memory afterwards — like the time when a visitor from America discovered in the Potstill Bar that another man in the same group was his second cousin from Ulster. Before that day they had never met!''

There is also an international code in the way people drink. ''Some Americans want tall glasses, with ice and lemon or soda water and only a faint flavour of whiskey. Most Californians sip their *Old Bushmills*, and have water in a separate glass. The Germans like it neat, but the French add water. Other visitors ask for lemonade with *Old Bushmills*, but we are trying to teach them the proper way!'' Jimmy has his own strict rule. ''Whiskey is made for sipping. If it is taken too quickly it gets to the root of all the wrong places!''

A speciality is Jimmy's ''Hot Bush''. This is brewed in a gleaming copper container that has pride of place on the counter of the bar. He heats the equivalent of two whiskey-bottles of water, with cloves and lemon and then drops in a bottle of *Old Bushmills*. Sugar is added and the ''Hot Bush'' is warm enough to dispel the vapours of the mistiest Antrim day.

There has been a remarkable range of visitors down the years, ''Caravanners, students, Round Tablers, Lions, rugby clubs, Rotarians, choirs, housewives, pensioners, businessmen, motor-cyclists, cyclists, hitch-hikers, people from thousands of miles away and people from just down the road. We've had everybody and everything, including the band of the U.S. Fleet. They came and played when the U.S. Navy base at Londonderry was closed. Boy that was some party! We've had choirs from Wales, choirs from Austria, singers, musicians, people who are the centre of attention and people who are happy to join in the fun from the sidelines. We've had some great times in the Potstill Bar!''

The walls are a silent witness to the chatter and chink as people pause, briefly or otherwise, to absorb something of the atmosphere and the character of the world's oldest whiskey Distillery. The plaques are a tangible reminder of the ghosts of the past, and the names tell their own stories — Troon Bowling Club, the Belgian Resistance Movement, plaques from Canada, from Singapore, from New Zealand and Zimbabwe, from a Peace Community nearby, from Kentucky, and California, and from all parts of the world. These *Old Bushmills* people move through the Distillery like the river of life itself.

Character

The Potstill Bar was formerly a fuel store which housed peat and then coal for firing the old kilns. Today it has become a bridge between old and new. It is more than a unique bar. It is a museum, a tourist centre and reminder of the long history of *Old Bushmills* since Sir Thomas Phillips was granted the licence to distil, in the vastly different circumstances of 1608. The Potstill Bar, like *Old Bushmills* itself has its own character. It is little wonder that tourist awards have been flooding in — a special commendation in the British Airways Tourism Endeavour Awards for ''providing a first-class reception centre and superb hospitality''; and a certificate of

The "Old Bushmills" open-topped bus is a familiar sight ferrying tourists in North Antrim. It carried the Northern Ireland soccer team on a victorious journey through Belfast after its outstanding success in the 1982 World Cup in Spain.

"In my boyhood days you made your own fun. There was no television, like today. We played football, we swam in the steeps of the Distillery, we went bird-nesting, and fishing. My first rod was a ten-foot length of bamboo, and it cost me sixpence! That was two weeks' pocket-money. We used to go down to the sea at ebb tide and collect limpets to use for baiting the hooks. The first fish I caught was a whopping nine pounds — it was well-hooked, but I was hooked for life! I've been a keen fisherman since. There's a special challenge in trying to outwit a noble species of fish like a salmon, but even when I'm not fishing, there's a great peace up there by the banks of a river, watching nature, noticing how things change from one season to another. I've always been a great outdoors man."

Jimmy recalls the plain food of his youth. "There was soup, broth, roast rabbit and roast hare. People kept their own chickens, and a plump boiling fowl cost a shilling. A local delicacy was eel soused in vinegar. There was plenty of salmon in the "Bush", and practically everyone grew Sharpe's Express potatoes. It was a tradition to have new potatoes and salmon on June 12th every year."

Christmas

"At Christmas there was carol singing and rhyming, with the "mummers." Some of the local farmers would invite you to their house for a soda scone and a drink of buttermilk. In the early days the family of a man working in the Distillery got a quart of whiskey at Christmas, and a turkey or a goose. A turkey was a luxury, and a goose cost five shillings, but some people couldn't afford even that.

"In the summer people would go to the Auld Lammas Fair in Ballycastle. It was 2/6 return by bus, but many of us went on our bikes and back again. Some would go in a pony and trap. There was a great holiday atmosphere, a sense of occasion. It was also a good place for a bargain, and many's a man bought his good suit there."

In those days people made their own entertainment. "There were games like draughts and darts, and if someone had a gramophone they could have filled the house with neighbours listening and dancing to Scottish country music. There was a great feeling of belonging to a community."

When Jimmy Kane left school he worked with an engineering firm and later as a driver before joining *Old Bushmills* in 1945. "When I came here first they were making very little whiskey. It was just at the end of the war and barley was still scarce. They needed it for food. In 1946 we made whiskey for only six weeks. It was 17 weeks the next year, and around 26 weeks by 1948. Then in the 'silent season' we did all the maintenance jobs around the place."

Driver

"I drove the *Old Bushmills* lorry, mainly to Belfast, though I also carried coal and turf to the Distillery. I remember setting off in an open-backed lorry at 5.30 in the morning to be in time to start at Coleraine. That was in our own time, if you don't mind! Sometimes we were in such a hurry that I was more afraid of being stopped by the police for low-flying rather than speeding!"

Jimmy remembers the characters around the Distillery. "The older men hated change. They would always say to you 'This system did me my day, why do you have to go and change it?' There was great skill in those days. A man would know how just when to run off a still, by sheer instinct and experience. If he got it wrong, the still would collapse like tissue paper, and there was a great respect for a man who never 'collapsed a still.' People took a great pride in their work. They polished the still until it shone. There was one old man of over 70 who used to pat the still every Friday before he left work and say 'You'll miss me when I'm gone!'

"They were hard days, but they were happy. The firm was a bit tight-fisted, but the atmosphere was leisurely. You were expected to do the best you could, but you were never pushed for time. Things have changed, now a lot of it's finger-tip control. Conditions are better, but I wonder sometimes if people are that much happier. We didn't have much, and there wasn't much education, but we had an awful lot of experience, and pride in making *Old Bushmills* the best that it could be."

There is a silence. Jimmy stops talking, and the ghosts of the past mingle with the present. Jimmy's family is part of the *Old Bushmills* history in the making. His wife has been a cleaner at the Distillery, his eldest son Johnny and two grandsons are coopers, his son-in-law works in the bottling hall, his daughter is also a guide and another daughter has been a secretary. The tradition now spans three generations.

Jimmy Kane, who was born within the shadow of "Old Bushmills", has guided many thousands of visitors around the Distillery. Jimmy is also a keen fisherman. "There's a special challenge in trying to outwit a noble species like a salmon."

Sammy McCallum followed his father and uncle who both worked at "Old Bushmills". When Sammy worked as a maltsman he was featured in a special series of advertisements, as seen here. Later he became a member of the Distillery's security staff.

Security

This tradition has been grounded partly in job security. Johnny Kane says "There was always the feeling that once you got into the Distillery, you were set for life. I went in straight from school, and I remember that my first wages weren't very big — something like 27/- or 28/- a week! Some of the old boys were great story-tellers. It was like a concert — you never knew how the days slipped by." Like his father, Johnny Kane also has a great love for nature and for the outdoors. "My grandfather used to keep game fowl and greyhounds. I love walking in the fresh air with just the dog for company. There's a great quietness about nature. I wouldn't have minded being a game-keeper!" In the event, Johnny Kane has spent his working life among the oaks and the barrels and the cooperage of the Distillery. "Even for a teetotaller like myself there's a special atmosphere and a lovely whiff from the oak casks."

The family tradition permeates *Old Bushmills*. Sammy McCallum followed his father and his uncle who both worked in the Distillery. "As a boy I used to carry my father's 'piece' or snack to him at work — a wee can of tea and a few sandwiches. Those were the days when they worked a 12-hour shift, six days a week. A bell at the Distillery was rung at certain hours, and it was so regular that the local farmers set their watches by it.

"There was a bell at 6.00 a.m. then one at 8.00 a.m. for breakfast, another to re-start at 9.00 a.m., a bell at 1.00 p.m. for lunch, another an hour later to restart, and a bell at six in the evening. There were no 'alarm calls' on the telephone in those days. A man called Wee Jimmy Watton used to be on the night-watch, and when he had finished early in the morning he would take an old fishing-rod and tap the windows of the houses to wake people up in time to get to their work!"

"I remember when the 8.00 a.m. bell rang, my mother would say 'Your father's on his way,' and she would be getting ready his breakfast, maybe a fry with home-baked soda. There wasn't much money. He had about £4 for a 72-hour week. The rent was maybe 1/- or 2/- a week. Times were hard financially, but we were happy. The children went barefoot in the summer-time but nobody felt deprived. We were all the same, and going barefoot seemed the natural thing to do.

Good Job

Sammy went to the local primary school. "My ambition always was to go into the Distillery. It was regarded as a good job, and steady. Once you were in, you were made for life. It was my father who got me in, and my first job was turning the malt floor. It was hard work, but there was a great pride in the work, keeping the malt level and spreading it out nicely. All the older men had great skill — my father, my uncle Robert, Tom Garvan, Davy Nicholl, John Walsh. There were great maltsmen at *Old Bushmills*.

"I used to get very tired at work until I became adjusted to it. I can remember the sweat running off us as we 'turned' a malt floor. I liked getting up early for the 6.00 a.m. shift. My wife would get up about 5.00 a.m. to provide a cooked breakfast, and at 5.30 a.m. the manager Mr. Morrison was at the gates to see that everybody was in on time. In those days there were not the same holidays, and I can remember working on a Christmas morning, rolling the barrels down the yard with the ice coming off your fingers. Mind you, there was always a great 'nip' of *Old Bushmills* on Christmas Day to help you on your way!"

Sammy McCallum worked for many years in the Tun Room as a brewer, before joining the security department. He was featured in a series of newspaper and magazine advertisements in the mid-Sixties which portrayed the work of certain employees in the Distillery. Part of the copy reads "He's the brewer: and the brewer is a key man wherever whiskey is made. He brews the malt liquour from which the whiskey is distilled. And the job is extremely exact . . ."

Some twenty years later, and after nearly forty years experience in *Old Bushmills*, Sammy McCallum reflects; "Money was tight, but money was tight everywhere. Conditions have definitely improved. Life in the Distillery is like life anywhere else — it's what you make it!"

Old Boys

Another man with long experience is Emuel McCallum, who works as a boilerman. "My uncle Tommy spent all his working life in the Distillery. He was a foreman in the malt barns, but I remember him telling me about carrying bricks with a horse and cart from Portrush to build the Pagoda Towers. That must have been at the turn of the century, maybe about 1912!"

Emuel began working in the malt barns, and he recalls some of the old characters. "There was Big Ben Johnston, the stillman, and Willie Verner. Then there were two old boys who always worked the night-shift, and the next morning they would knock up the people to go to their job in the flax-mill. You could hear the clip-clop of their boots as they walked down the street in the early morning.

"People in the flax-mill worked from 7.30 a.m. to 7.30 p.m. One of the great advantages was to get 'showes' which were the remnants of the flax. If you burned them together with peat it made a great fire all night."

There were other characters around the Distillery. "Sam Deane was a plasterer. He was known as 'Pawkle'. It was a great place for nick-names. And there was Hamilton Cooper, who was a joiner. He and 'Pawkle' Dean were terrific tradesmen. You can see their work around the Distillery to this very day."

Emuel McCallum worked at one time as a conductor on the famous Causeway Tram. "The fare was 1/9 return from Portrush to the Causeway. She was slow but you had a good chance to breathe the fresh air and to take a look at the countryside. There were some bad days when the weather was awful, but generally I remember the good times. And very often the tram was packed. You could hardly get on to it just before tea-time when people wanted to catch the Portrush train back to Belfast!"

Bare Feet

Like other men at *Old Bushmills* Emuel remembers the days as children when they ran about in bare feet and made their own entertainment. "The food wasn't the same. You were lucky to get meat, not like today when it seems to be more plentiful. Money was tighter but there was a good community spirit. There was a great sense of law and order, and the local policeman, Constable McMahon, ruled with an iron hand. If you did something wrong he would give you a clout on the ear, and if you went home complainin' to your parents and told them what had happened you were likely to get a clip on the other ear as well!"

"The people today have more, but I wonder if they are as happy . . ."

In every business and in nearly all walks of life there is a wistfulness about the best of the past and a temptation to talk about the "good old days." This is all part of the modern world where conformity tends to erode individuality. Perhaps it is also part of the human condition where many people believe that the heroes of their past were as large as life, and perhaps even larger; where the weather was nearly always good; and where there was a kind of universal innocence that was unpolluted by the haste and materialism of much of the modern age.

Nevertheless, realism dictates that there should be a balanced view, that there were also the "bad old days" when wages were low, jobs could be uncertain, health care was patchy, and when luxuries of life were few. Material conditions have improved. Housing and health facilities have changed for the better. It does not follow, however, that improving the conditions necessarily meet an individual's deepest personal needs, but given a choice between the realities of the present and a certain romanticism about the past it is doubtful if a majority would turn back the clock, even if they could. There is an innate quality about life, whether in the "good" or "bad" old days or in the present which is available to those who know how to appreciate it.

Last Words

Fittingly, the last words should be left to a lady who personifies the service that women have provided in the background for generations of *Old Bushmills* employees, and more recently in the work of the Distillery itself. Mrs. Ebbie Morrow, is the Supervisor in the Bottling Hall. She and her family have connections *with Old Bushmills* for almost a quarter of a century.

Her first husband, Sandy Kane, died at the age of 47. For more than 20 years he had worked in the Distillery, and he was featured in the Sixties advertising campaign which concentrated on *Old Bushmills* employees. Part of the advertisement read; "Sandy Kane, maltster, controls a living, biological process. He lays the barley down in the warm air of the maltroom. He refreshes the grain with the, cool, clear water of Antrim, and he watches it germinate and grow. When it's ready, and exactly when is a secret that is his alone, he gives the word; the malt, which the

Emuel McCallum, in the "Old Bushmills" boiler-room. He remembered his Uncle Tommy who carried bricks with a horse and cart to help build the Distillery's Pagoda Towers, at the turn of the century.

Mrs. Ebbie Morrow, Supervisor in the Bottling Hall at the Distillery. "I feel a great sense of loyalty to Old Bushmills. It gave us security, identity, steady pay, and pride."

barley has become, is taken away to be dried over a peat fire."

Ebbie, who is now married to a Mr. Samuel Morrow, recalls how she felt when her first husband, Sandy, was given a job in the Distillery.

"We were married young — I was only 16 — and work was hard to come by. My husband would be employed for short periods by local farmers and then he would be back on the dole. It was very hard to plan ahead, especially when there was no way of knowing how much money was coming in."

"When Sandy got a job with *Old Bushmills* it was a Godsend. It was hard work, but he was at least dry and indoors, there was a steady wage, and we could begin to plan ahead a bit. And things gradually improved. I'm not one who talks much about the "good old days." The working people are now just beginning to get on their feet. In the past you had to watch every penny you spent. Now I have carpets in my home and I can afford a car. I didn't have those in the "good old days!"

"When Sandy took ill one of his great regrets was that he might have to leave his job when things were improving so much. A great deal of the drudgery had gone out of it, and it was much more a case of push-button control. Sadly, he was not to live on to enjoy the benefits of the new techniques.

"I must say that I feel a real sense of loyalty to *Old Bushmills*. It gave us security, identity, steady pay and a feeling of pride. Times have been hard, particularly recently in the worldwide recession, but throughout the ups and downs of all the years *Old Bushmills* has gone on. And you have the feeling that no matter what happens, it will still be there. It really is a special place. After all, its the oldest whiskey Distillery in the world!"

THE "OLD BUSHMILLS" DISTILLERY CO. LTD.
TRADE MARK
1608

Acknowledgements

It would require a separate chapter to thank all those who helped to make this book a reality. Covering as it does nearly 400 years, the narrative owes a debt to individuals in the past as well as the present. Previous generations have left layers of history, like the slow and silent build-up of a coral reef that takes a shape and an identity of its own. It has been my privilege to study this past and also to provide another layer for observers of the future.

One man deserving of special recognition is Bill McCourt, who asked me to write this book. To the extent that he was anxious to gather together all the known history of "Old Bushmills" to mark the 375th anniversary, and also to record the oral and factual history of passing generations before it was too late, this volume is largely his original idea. During the fascinating but exacting process of developing a concept into a reality, I found his enthusiasm infectious, his encouragement constant and his constructive criticism (coming from a man with a love for books) both challenging and helpful.

Clair Balmer provided immense support and her "little black book" of dates, places, times, amendments, suggestions, and queries was an essential key to the manuscript itself. Her patience, interest and ideas were invaluable. John Belshaw of Universities Press (Belfast) was a major source of help and technical advice, as he transformed the manuscript and pictures into a book with a shape and a momentum. Last, but not least, in this small group of people who lived closely with the book is Hilary McCreary, who once again drew a deep breath and allowed me to get on with it, despite other pressing matters. Her silent but significant contribution is there, between the lines.

I would also like to thank Willie MacKay for giving up several of his summer Saturdays to help simplify the technicalities of production and also for helping to read the proofs, and Richard Burrows for his supportive interest and his eye for detail.

Indebted

Many other people have made a contribution. I am indebted to Dan MacLaughlin for his wit, insight and historical knowledge, particularly concerning the chapter on Coleraine; Hugh Alexander Boyd of Ballycastle who was most helpful and provided a number of important historical signposts along the way; Trevor Parkhill of the

Public Record Office of Northern Ireland, for unravelling some of the historical knots of the "Old Bushmills" story in the 19th century; Charles Brett for providing access to relevant documents; the Macnaghten family for permission to quote from their correspondence, George Cameron for guiding me through the maze of business and income tax papers in the early 20th century; Granville Nugent and John MacLennan for explaining the mysteries of malting and blending; Jimmy Kane for his anecdotes and recollections; and to all those "Old Bushmills" employees past and present who are mentioned in the narrative. Without their help, the story of "Old Bushmills" would be the poorer.

An important dimension to "Old Bushmills" has been its family history. This was particularly the case with the Boyds of Belfast and I am most grateful to Mrs. Janet Boyd in particular and to her son Kenneth for providing a wealth of oral, written and photographic material concerning that era.

The chapter outlining the "American Connection" was made possible by people in the United States who provided not only material but who also helped to open doors that otherwise might have remained closed for ever. These include Bill Street and Ron Ralph in Kentucky, Sol Abeles in New York and Morris Rosen in Miami. In this context I am particularly grateful to Mrs. Sallye Kaplan, whose hospitality to me in Florida was as unbounded as her supply of anecdotes, photographs and written material was significant.

Illustrations

A book of this nature relies for its presentation on the quality of its illustrations. I would like, therefore, to record my thanks to James MacIntyre for his drawings and to John Currie and Wilfred Green for their photography. The Northern Ireland Tourist Board was extremely helpful, not least in supplying some outstanding photographs, which show the natural beauty of the homeland of "Old Bushmills."

Every author engaged on a project of this nature depends greatly on the help from individuals and institutions. I would like, therefore, to record the courteous assistance given to me by the staff of the Ulster Museum, the Ulster Folk and Transport Museum, the Public Record Office of Northern Ireland, the National Trust, the Linen Hall Library, the Belfast Central Library, Coleraine County Library, and the librarian and staff of the "Belfast Telegraph." I should also like to thank the editors of the "Belfast Telegraph," the "News Letter," "The Observer," and others at home and abroad for the use of extracts from their publications. A special word of thanks is due also to the "Coleraine Chronicle" for its faithful record of contemporary history, and for its help in the present.

I have also made use of writings and documents from many other sources, which are of relevance to "Old Bushmills" and to the industry itself. These contributions are acknowledged in the narrative and I record my gratitude to the authors and publishers mentioned. I am also most grateful to Helen Gregg and Sheelagh Croskery for typing various sections of the manuscript, with cheerfulness and efficiency.

Pleasure

While it is always a pleasure to record thanks, there is a fear at the back of my mind that I will omit to mention a person or persons who proved to be most helpful. This may well happen, life being what it is! But there may be some consolation in knowing that such thanks will indeed be rendered by the author, and not without pain, during some sleepless night when he remembers those whom he had inadvertently overlooked. Realistically, no list of acknowledgements would be complete without a reference to Sir Thomas Phillips himself, who started it all 375 years ago. I wonder what he would make of the story of "Old Bushmills" today. Finally, this book has given me a new insight into big business and local history — as well as providing an entirely new dimension to "proof reading!" I have much enjoyed the world of "Old Bushmills" and the blending of people, places and events to produce the "Spirit of the Age."

Picture Credits

Northern Ireland Tourist Board — back cover, pages 2, 5, 8, 9, 12, 24, 35, 153.
Ulster Museum — pages 7 (Golden Salamander), 27 and 28 (Robert John Welch prints), 30, 47, 76, 124, 126-7.
Ulster Folk and Transport Museum — pages 20, 21, 24, 176.
Public Record Office of Northern Ireland — page 45 (T22 92/3).
National Maritime Museum, Greenwich — page 7 (Spanish Galleass).
National Trust — page 4.
National Library of Ireland — page 58.
Coleraine County Library — pages 193, 199 (Old Cafe), 204, 207.
"Coleraine Chronicle" — pages 27, 203.
"Daily Mirror" — page 220.
Belfast Telegraph" — page 92.
"Belfast News Letter" — pages 104, 190.
"Daily Mail" — page 131.
"Kansas Beverage News" — page 134.
Thomas Yoseloff, New York and London — page 197.
The "Old Bushmills" Distillery Co. Ltd. — Front cover, pages 69, 92, 93, 94, 115, 131, 155, 158-9, 164-5, 172, 176, 177, 184, 186, 212.
Brown-Forman Distillers Corporation, Kentucky — page 130.
The Late Jimmy Magowan Collection, Ballycastle — page 49.
The Boyd Family — pages 77, 79, 82, 88, 89, 91, 97, 99, 140
John Currie — pages 28, 34, 36, 56, 57, 63, 64, 65, 66, 68, 70, 71, 74, 86, 128, 131, 136, 145 (Glass Figure), 146, 154, 160, 175, 180, 187, 202, 203, 216, 222, 223, 226, 227.
Wilfred Green — pages 77, 79, 82, 99, 101, 104, 150, (Granville Nugent), 157, (Permission BBC), pages 185, 190, 214, 218.
James MacIntyre-Drawings on pages 38, 41, 50, 55, 59, 61.
Mrs. Kaplan — pages 132, 133, 141.
The Macnaghten Family — page 23
Morris Rosen — page 134.
Michael Joseph — Front Cover, pages 155
Bill McCourt — pages 14, 16, 114, 120, 145 (Dolmen), 168, 170, 181, 182, 199 (New Restaurant), 211, 212 (Coleraine Distillery).
Alf McCreary — pages 6, 33, 111, 137, 148.